PLACE MATTERS

"Bill and Coz have earned the right to introduce us to Common Grace in Philly. They both came from afar, and stayed! Here they combine years of research and passion to grab and inspire a new generation of students in schools and frontline ministries. They put names on complex realities. Common Grace has one of the finest learning labs in the world, and hosts of young ministry leaders that need to see it. In the words of that great Philly theologian, Rocky, 'Go for it.'"

—Ray Bakke
Executive Director, International Urban Associates
Author of *The Urban Christian*

"*Place Matters* is an insightful and highly practical guide to how to engage and effectively minister in an urban (or really any) setting. It shows us the power of taking the time and care to listen to and learn from the city, as well as the power of appropriately contextualized and connected action."

—Jeffrey Bass
Executive Director, Emmanuel Gospel Center

"This book is a call to 'outsiders' to see what God is doing in the city through a different lens. Then it takes a breath in order to call 'insiders' to reach their city for Christ with a different approach. I enjoyed Coz and Bill's paradigm-shifting perspective on how place matters. Those of you who are serious about understanding the urban dynamics of the cities God has called you to reach would do well to let this book provoke your heart and stimulate your mind."

—Jamie Centeno
Author of *Heavolution* and *Milk & Honey*
Chief servant @ IN THE LIGHT

"This book reminds me of seminary departments that pride themselves on having a healthy practical theology department. *Place Matters* is really practical for every local ministry seeing itself as a place for God's kingdom to come with disciple making as the goal to be achieved. *Place Matters* can be used as a manual for training in effective twenty-first century urban ministry."

—Dr. Lawrence F. Chiles
Professor, Lancaster Bible College, Philadelphia, PA

"At a time when generic brands, blanket coverage, and one-size-fits-all are common, Krispin and Crosscombe prove that in ministry your particular place matters. They provide a challenging, biblical framework to understand your neighborhood and a street-smart toolbox to unpack the need for the gospel in your community. This is a book that I wish I had in my hand before I entered pastoral ministry, especially before I began church planting."

—Bruce Finn
Church Planting Coordinator, Metro Phila. Church Planting Partnership
Pastor of Missions, Covenant Church, Doylestown, PA

"In *Place Matters*, Bill Krispin and Coz Crosscombe speak from experience in describing the type of ministry needed to grow the Christian faith at a kingdom level in our complex contemporary world. This book contains much of their wisdom and practical personal experience—laced with humility and vulnerability—and gives many examples of various kingdom-minded ministries that have been working together over decades in Philly, and they tie it all together on a strongly biblical foundation. This book helps the reader understand how Christianity can grow in an entire city."

—Doug and Judy Hall
Consultants, Living System Ministry
Emmanuel Gospel Center

"Coz Crosscombe and Bill Krispin have produced an extremely accessible book on what a healthy urban church looks like. There are many years of street-level experience packed in this highly readable book. Highly recommended."

—Tim Keller
Pastor Emeritus, Redeemer Presbyterian Churches of New York City

"I am honored to write my observations about this book, *Place Matters*. Both Bill Krispin and Coz Crosscombe have painted a beautiful picture of the true purpose of the body of Christ. That purpose is to multiply and reach the surrounding communities. This is an exciting book to read. It is practical and yet has enough theology to satisfy the student. It is life applicable without being overstated. Most of all, it challenges those in leadership to take a hard look at the purpose and function of the local church. This book will inspire church leaders to redefine the mission of the church and work together instead of apart."

—Bishop Eric Lambert Jr.
Presiding Bishop, Bethel Deliverance International Fellowship of Churches
Pastor, Bethel Deliverance International Church

"When I first moved to Philly to plant Epiphany Fellowship, I asked who I should talk to for a working knowledge of my context. Bill Krispin's name was at the top of the list! He is a veteran consultant on urban missions. He has aided scores of leaders in getting a head start on their understanding of gospel engagement in Philadelphia. Drs. William Krispin and Coz Crosscombe are trusted leaders in the Delaware Valley and are known for their urban demographical information for planters and urban missionaries. Pick up this book and learn what is in your context and how to approach gospel ministry in it."

—Dr. Eric M. Mason
Lead Pastor, Epiphany Fellowship Church

"For decades, urban ministry practitioners, especially those who have served in metro Philadelphia, have been gleaning from the experience-soaked wisdom of Bill Krispin and Coz Crosscombe. Finally, their wisdom encased in a book! There is treasure here, not the least of which is the reminder that true transformation happens through long-term commitment to a place. This and many other nuggets provide both the inspiration and the practical tools for the church that desires to fulfill its missional call in the city and beyond."

—Al Tizon
Executive Minister, Serve Globally
Evangelical Covenant Church

"In the incarnation, Jesus left a realm in which time and space had no consequence in order to live at a particular time, in a particular place, with a particular people. Coz and Bill help us to dive into the most important work of our time, learning to be the tangible presence of Christ in the neighborhood to which God has sent us."

—JR Woodward
National Director, V3 Church Planting Movement
Author, *Creating a Missional Culture*; Coauthor, *The Church as Movement*

"*Place Matters* calls attention to key issues that must not be ignored if a church is to be fruitful in its ministry and witness. This is a book that is born out of biblical conviction and tested against years of ministry experience in a diversity of contexts, communities, and cultures."

—Dwight Yoo
Senior Pastor, Renewal Presbyterian Church, Philadelphia, PA

PLACE MATTERS

PLACE MATTERS

THE **CHURCH** FOR THE **COMMUNITY**

COZ CROSSCOMBE
AND **BILL KRISPIN**

PUBLICATIONS

Fort Washington, PA 19034

Place Matters
Published by CLC Publications

U.S.A.
P.O. Box 1449, Fort Washington, PA 19034

UNITED KINGDOM
CLC International (UK)
Unit 5, Glendale Avenue, Sandycroft, Flintshire, CH5 2QP

Printed in the United States of America

ISBN (paperback): 978-1-61958-262-0
ISBN (e-book): 978-1-61958-263-7

Cover design by Mitch Bolton.

DEDICATION

Coz:
To those unlikely people in unlikely spaces doing the remarkable work of our Lord while receiving little to no earthly attention—you form the foundation of God's work in hard places. Your stories need to be told to inspire the rest of us onward.

Bill:
This book is dedicated to those close to me who have most shaped and influenced my life and thought—my wife of fifty years, Mary, and our five children: Karen, Jonathan, Timothy, Rebecca, and Elizabeth, along with their spouses and our fifteen grandchildren. Our extended family also includes our church family at Pilgrim Presbyterian in Philadelphia and the Christ Fellowship in Valdosta, Georgia, where we spend the winter months.

CONTENTS

ACKNOWLEDGMENTS

So many people have contributed significantly to my understanding of local communities, from formal educators in my life—Ray Bakke, Doug Hall, Jeff Bass, Eldin Villafane, Bobby Bose, Kris Rocke, Manny Ortiz, Joel Van Dyke, and Mark Sarracino—to those teaching me on the streets of those communities—Gene Wright, Bo Nixon, Alex Wright, Lou Centeno, Hector Espinosa, Tony Gonzalez, Doug Logan, Larry Smith, Nes Espinosa, Andres Fajardo, Zack Ritvalsky, Charles Zimmerman, and Roberto Vargas. I am grateful to each one of you.

I also want to thank ministry teams with whom I have had the opportunity to serve. They have poured into my life, particularly at Young Life in Australia, Bethel Temple Community Bible Church, Esperanza Health Center, the Simple Way, and Spirit and Truth Fellowship in the United States. Thanks also to Dr. Williams and Dr. Toews at Cairn University for their support as I wrote this book.

Most of all, I want to thank my family—Joyce, Saiyeh, Melanie, Emma, and Tony—who teach me new ways to see our community, challenge my conceptions, and overcome what seem to be impossible obstacles. You live out what I can often only conceptualize.

—Coz

There are so many people I need to thank. They include the family of Center for Urban Theological Studies (CUTS), students I have taught and who have taught me much of what I know about Philadelphia ministry. I also want to thank those who have supported and mentored me over the years: Dr. Willie Richardson, Dr. Bill Grier, Dr. Wesley Pinnock, Bishop Eric Ricks, and, last but not least, Dr. Bob DeMoss, who taught and encouraged me to lead my family during its younger years. Your respective influences are all deep and profound. I also want to thank the staff of CLC who made this book possible: David Almack, Erika Cobb (whose support and patient prodding kept things moving), and Becky English (whose editorial assistance turned a very rough manuscript into a special jewel).

—Bill

PREFACE

For many years, our friends have encouraged us to write a book together. When we first met, almost twenty years ago, Bill was a seminary-trained urban practitioner known for his Bible teaching and understanding of the history of the greater Philadelphia area. I wasn't much of a reader. I was more identified by my no-nonsense, boots-on-the-ground approach to life and ministry in an urban setting. Our common love for the city of Philly and passion for incarnational urban ministry drew us together, and our differing gifts have challenged us both and helped us grow together as we lived among and served people in our local communities.

Over the last century, the American church has moved from a parish ministry to a regional, building-centered, program-focused ministry. The result is that people often worship in locations somewhat distant from their own neighborhoods, and local communities are left without a vital incarnational witness to the transforming gospel of Jesus Christ. But the local community around a church actually matters! If we as believers can understand our own communities, we can build connections to effectively carry out God's calling in them.

As we studied trends and noticed this growing problem, we decided to start a ministry in 2009 called Common Grace Inc. with our friend Nes Espinosa. Our goal was to understand and nurture Christianity in Philadelphia by building partnerships between churches and ministries across neighborhoods. In the past eight years, we have interacted with many ministry models, watched as trends came and went, and witnessed communities transform. All of this has reinforced our belief that place matters.

My wife, Joyce, and I have lived and served in north Philadelphia for almost two decades. I am an Australian and have served with Young Life, Bethel Temple, and Wyoming Avenue Baptist, where I ministered with youth and led economic and community development. Joyce is a Pennsylvania girl. A graduate of Eastern University, she served as a school teacher in southwest Philly and the Dominican Republic before landing in north Philadelphia. She has been a pioneer for women coming into the community, worked extensively in children's ministry, and now focuses on mentoring women. We have three daughters—Saiyeh, Melanie, and Emma—and a son, Tony David Luis. Each of our kids has a growing love and understanding of Philadelphia, its poverty, and its special place in God's kingdom.

—Coz

I have been involved in Philadelphia urban ministry for forty-four years. Born and raised on the north side of Chicago, I came to Westminster Seminary in 1965 with the intent of eventually returning to my hometown. But in 1967, Jack Miller challenged me to take up urban ministry in Philadelphia. So following an internship at Tenth Presbyterian, I moved with my wife, Mary, to south Philadelphia to plant Emmanuel Chapel as an Orthodox Presbyterian congregation. All five of our children were born during these years. Early on, I got involved in a prayer group of Philadelphia pastors, who initiated the Westminster Saturday Seminar. That became the Center for Urban Theological Studies (CUTS) in 1978, where I served as executive director for nearly twenty years. I have also served as the pastor of Pilgrim Church in the Roxborough/Manayunk section of Philadelphia and been executive director of CityNet Ministries for planting churches in our city and region. Now in my retirement, I serve as a senior research fellow for Common Grace.

Both of us are often asked to help people understand the communities in Philadelphia, and other cities in the United States and around the world. Whether we have worked with new church planters, seasoned pastors, relocating families, or academic students, we have seen a need to help people understand the community where they are or will be ministering. We have at times been heartbroken, watching individuals and ministries fail in the mission to make disciples because they had little understanding or connection to the place where they are located. We have also been encouraged and challenged by unlikely people serving in unlikely places all around the world. Their work should inspire us all.

In this book, we lay out a theology of place, the foundation from which all ministry flows. We give examples of how we have seen people living intentionally in their places, and we offer long-term analysis of what works and what doesn't. We also give tools and techniques to take these ideas from theory to reality. We can say with full confidence that incarnational living really does work.

Our central passion in writing this book is to encourage churches and church planters to engage their surrounding

communities with the gospel. This book isn't for someone looking to grow numbers in their ministry, as there are plenty of
books out there on how to attract people. It is for people who
want to see kingdom growth—new disciples being made rather
than Christians simply moving from one church to another.

This book does not stand alone. We are always encouraged to
see what an incredibly diverse range of people and ministries have
been effective in community-based ministry—people not restricted by a particular doctrine or stylized practice but motivated by a
commitment to love every person as Christ has called us to.

—Bill

No one church has all the gifts and resources needed to transform the communities of Philadelphia or any other city. Philadelphia is a city of 1.5 million people, made up of hundreds of
microcommunities, each functioning as part of the whole yet
still distinct from each other. Each of these communities must
be reached by local churches if we are to see transformation
happen. It is only as we work together as the whole body of
Christ that we can carry out the Great Commission in our local
communities. This is why we assist ministries in their work to
cooperate with each other and reach the urban community by
connecting, supporting, and mobilizing church and community
leaders as they seek to spread the gospel and address the needs of
their communities. We encourage you to read broadly and, even
more, to visit and engage with others in ministry in your area.
Don't consider just the new and flashy work or the pastor on
the speaking circuit, but dig deep into your community to find
those serving without attention.

This book is a mix of strategic principles for engaging in community-based ministry and biblical exposition on key passages

related to the incarnational ministry modeled by Christ. We use stories to illustrate the outworking of these principles and passages. We have been effectively teaching these techniques (Bill for more than fifty years, Coz for not quite so long) and applying them in a diverse range of communities. We hope we can impart some of this knowledge so that you, in turn, will be better equipped to do the most blessed work of loving those around you.

Ultimately, our hope is that whether you are a church planter, a pastor, or a ministry leader, you will be challenged to lead your church to connect with your surrounding community in multiple ways. We look forward to hearing your stories of community engagement. Please email your stories to Commongracephilly@gmail.com. Our heart's prayer is that every man, woman, and child in your surrounding community will have multiple opportunities to see, hear, and be touched by the powerful, life-transforming gospel of Jesus Christ.

PART 1

THE CALL—LIVING THE GOSPEL IN OUR COMMUNITIES

1

BEING CHURCH IN THE COMMUNITY

When you think of your calling and vision for ministry, what comes to your mind? Do you think of your microworld—that is, those in your local church— or do you look more broadly at the macroworld made up of your neighborhood, your city, and your personal world where you live every day?

Christ calls us to look not just at those who attend our local churches but also at the people we rub shoulders with on the sidewalk in front of our houses, in our neighborhood grocery stores, in the local parks where our kids play. When we stop and take a good look at our own communities, we realize that we are looking at a world that is lost, broken, and largely forgotten by the church.

This brokenness is why Jesus sent His disciples out into the communities around them.

> The Lord appointed seventy-two others and sent them two by two ahead of him to every town and

place where he was about to go. He told them, "The harvest is plentiful, but the workers are few. Ask the Lord of the harvest, therefore, to send out workers into his harvest field. Go! I am sending you out like lambs among wolves." (Luke 10:1–3)

Our local communities are vast, rich harvest fields. But this crop cannot be harvested without workers, many more than we have. We must pray to the Lord of the harvest to send workers into the harvest field. God wants a multiplicity of workers putting their lives to work, and the vision is larger than any one person or even one church can accomplish. God wants every man, woman, and child in the world around us to have multiple opportunities to hear, see, and be touched by the powerful gospel of Christ.[1] This is the message of our book.

As coauthors, we also live and minister in Philadelphia, a city of 1.5 million people within a larger metropolitan area of 6 million.[2] Someone who knows the statistics might say, "Your region has more than four thousand churches—one for every 1,500 people." But it is estimated that the average church in the United States has only 178 people in attendance on any given Sunday.[3] In Philly, that translates to only about 12 percent of the population. The harvest field is vast and ripe not just on the foreign mission field. It is vast and ripe right here in our Western communities. Who will work to harvest those in the areas directly around us?

That's the challenge and the opportunity, and they're bigger than any one of us. We need all the partners we can find and we need to work in concert with one another to engage in this harvest ministry. Are you ready to join the battle for the world?

KNOWING OUR COMMUNITIES

Whether you live in a challenged urban neighborhood, an expanding suburban community, or an area swarming with new city gentrifiers, we have to understand our local communities and the changes taking place in them if we want to have any chance of reaching them with the gospel.

I have lived in my neighborhood, northeast of Center City Philadelphia, for more than a decade. My local community, Frankford, is quite diverse, both ethnically and economically. And like many of Philadelphia's communities, it's changing.

When my family first moved here, we lived next door to a Grace Brethren church. Its building had once been a veteran's hall, although originally it had been one of the Frankford mansions. I'd walk past the back of that church, down through the park, and turn left onto Orthodox Street, and on the corner was "Seven Up"—the Seventh United Presbyterian Church. On the next corner was the large Methodist church and opposite that another old stone church. Then I'd pass the Quaker meeting hall, dating back to 1775. A block down and I encountered the El, Philadelphia's elevated transit line. Under the El in Frankford (never a pleasant place, especially after dark) were more large church buildings—Episcopal, Presbyterian, Baptist. Also nearby was the local Catholic church, boasting a large modern building with the requisite school attached.

Ten years later (years that don't feel as long as they were), the lot where the Methodist building stood is now vacant, the building having fallen down. "Seven Up" houses a small congregation from a Word of Faith church. The Brethren have shut down. The Catholic complex, including the school, was sold at auction. The Quakers run a school, Frankford Friends, but most of its students now come from outside our community. One stone church is occupied by an Indian Malankara congregation. Although our community is culturally diverse, this particular congregation drives in from other areas and they have put their building up for sale. You could take all the people who attend church on Sundays at the other traditional churches and fit them all in one small building. A really small building.

Frankford is a historical community. Frankford Avenue was once part of the King's Highway, one of the oldest ridge roads in America, and played a part in national history, including the Underground Railroad. Frankford has also been home to some of Philadelphia's historically significant black churches and white churches.

Today most of the churches in Frankford are quite small, sharing space with other churches or housed in storefronts. The huge old stone churches were built big, with parsonages attached or nearby, because they once had large congregations housed inside them. They didn't have parking lots because when they were built, their members walked to church. These churches anchored the community through growth and change and challenge. Now they are monuments or memorials to a time long past.

In the thirteen years or so that I lived in Kensington, a neighborhood about a mile south of Frankford, I saw almost every mainline denominational church close down or merge. On Allegheny Avenue, where I lived, every church building except the ones owned by the Catholic churches changed hands, some more than once.

WHAT'S HINDERING US?

The idea for Common Grace Inc. started when Bill imagined a group that could strategically work to facilitate church unification. Instead of coming to join, people would go out and see what God was already doing in urban communities and bring people together to reach those areas for Christ.

As we work with groups in Philadelphia and beyond, we are often amazed at how little local churches know about one another and especially how little new church planters know about the communities they have targeted for church plants. It's a given that people plant churches because they believe there is a need in a community. They can usually cite some statistic about the lack of a "real gospel presence" there, but few know the real story of the community and the church there.

This happens for many reasons. One is that pastors and church planters tend to be busy, driven by the needs they see in front of them and inspired to reach new people with the gospel. Another is that most church plants are given a three- to five-year window to be up and running and financially independent—a challenging goal to achieve, especially in complex and diverse communities—so church planters aren't easily afforded the time to settle into the community. Sometimes it is because people are arrogant in thinking that God talks only through them, their denomination, and their theological perspective.

The major reason, though, is that too often existing churches and church plants see themselves in competition for the small pool of existing believers who already attend church services. Church planters also compete for those who can be leaders and financial givers and help the churches grow and move forward.

They often do this without intent, though at times it is purposeful. They may think the existing churches are irrelevant, ineffective, not real Bible churches, or not missional enough. Instead of becoming strategic allies in the Kingdom with a common mission of reaching every man, woman, and child with the transforming gospel of Christ, churches and church planters often function as independent tribes, appearing at war with one another and failing to reach out to the people around them.

In the midst of this tribalism is the disturbing fact that fewer and fewer people are attending church in the United States. As we noted earlier, on any given Sunday in Philadelphia, Common Grace estimates that about 12 percent of the population is in church. That leaves 88 percent of the population outside the church. This is the dominant market share, so to speak. And these are the people we are called to reach.

Many blame the decline of the church on how we have entered the post-Christian age, or on the fact that millennials don't share the values of their parents, or that immigrants from non-Christian countries are coming to the West in far greater numbers. All these factors may be contributors to the decline of the church; but without a doubt, a large part of the problem is that local churches and church planters are woefully underprepared to understand the changing demographics of our communities, cities, counties, and country as a whole. When we don't understand who lives in our communities, we have little chance of reaching those people and that is when the statistics play out. Despite the waves of church planting that many are embracing today, there are more churches closing down than being planted in most of the country.

The world around us is continuously changing and we must learn to adapt to our ever-changing communities. Most church leaders have had some training in exegesis (or interpretation) of the Scriptures; but few know how to practice exegesis of their communities, let alone understand how to read and engage them.

In the following chapters, we lay out what we think are essential components to learning a community with the goal of reaching every person in a given neighborhood with the gospel. (We will use the term "neighborhood" to describe a specific geographic location and the term "community" to describe the connections between the people who live in a geographic location.) We will look at how a neighborhood is outlined; the spiritual, physical, and psychological boundaries that define that area; and how to build strategic alliances in our communities instead of creating competitors and enemies. We will cover how to embrace our communities, be part of building up their God-given assets, develop leaders, and steward what God has given each of us. This is all mandated by Jesus' command to "go and make disciples" (Matt. 28:19), and we will distinguish this from making converts or growing our own churches.

Undergirding this will be a theology of place—the idea that place matters.

COME BE WITH ME

Why does place matter? Does the gospel demand our presence in and for our local communities? Or are we truly more effective when we build large churches and attract an entire region of commutable people to our buildings because they fit the economic, racial, or social status that makes us feel most comfortable?

In the incarnation, Christ the living Word became flesh and lived among us.

> In the beginning was the Word, and the Word was with God, and the Word was God. . . . The Word became flesh and made his dwelling among us. We have seen his glory, the glory of the one and only Son, who came from the Father, full of grace and truth. . . . No one has ever seen God, but the one and only Son, who is himself God and is in closest relationship with the Father, has made him known. (John 1:1–18)

As the incarnational body of Christ today, the church is called to bring the presence and touch of Christ into our local communities. This doesn't mean just bringing the presence of Christ to a local church building or among a gathering of Christians but living out the very presence—the incarnation—of Christ in our neighborhoods.

John further amplifies this great truth by saying:

> That which was from the beginning, which we have heard, which we have seen with our eyes, which we have looked at and our hands have touched—this we proclaim concerning the Word of life. The life appeared; we have seen it and testify to it, and we proclaim to you the eternal life, which was with the Father and has appeared to us. We proclaim to you what we have seen and heard, so that you also may have fellowship with us. And our fellowship is with

the Father and with his Son, Jesus Christ. (1 John 1:1–3)

This fellowship is transformational both in our relationship to God and in our relationships with one another.

John says that they had seen and heard Jesus, that their hands had touched Him. This tells us that Jesus was up close and personal with His disciples and the masses He encountered. He didn't communicate with them in formal religious settings but interacted with them in daily, real-life situations. Jesus spent three years with His disciples on a daily basis.

Note further Jesus' calling of the first disciples in Matthew 4:18–22.

> As Jesus was walking beside the Sea of Galilee, he saw two brothers, Simon called Peter and his brother Andrew. They were casting a net into the lake, for they were fishermen. "Come, follow me," Jesus said, "and I will send you out to fish for people." At once they left their nets and followed him.
>
> Going on from there, he saw two other brothers, James son of Zebedee and his brother John. They were in a boat with their father Zebedee, preparing their nets. Jesus called them, and immediately they left the boat and their father and followed him.

"Come, follow Me" is another way of saying "Come, be with Me." The call to discipleship is a call to engagement with Christ in all of life. Seeing, touching, and hearing are all part of this process. Today we rarely know our fellow church attendees out-side of the formal worship setting on a Sunday morning. If we don't interact with each other in our local communities on a day-to-day basis, how will the unbelieving world ever see, hear, and be touched by Christ?

Place matters to God. Place always mattered to Jesus. The Gospel narratives distinguish the locations of Jesus and the dis-ciples throughout their writing. Jesus knew His local audience, and His message was directed toward that audience in such a way as to connect with the people. It mattered to Him whether He was in Jerusalem or Galilee. He chose His words and delivery differently depending on whether He was in Caesarea Philippi or Capernaum, Samaria or Jerusalem.

We see that the idea of place matters to God throughout the Old Testament as well, and is woven into our historical narrative as believers. From creation taking place in a garden to heaven being formed as an eternal city, where we are and what we do in each location matters.

PLACE MATTERS

In the past twenty-five years, we have seen a rise in attrac-tional regional churches that draw people from extended geo-graphic areas to their buildings. This kind of church does not connect well to its surrounding neighborhood or to the com-munities where most attendees live. Church life revolves around the building, and all or most of the church's resources and gifts are directed internally to those already attending. Why? Because it is a lot easier to attract people to upscale buildings and pro-gram-heavy, highly resourced churches than to meet people in our local neighborhoods and find ways to connect with them. And because, when it comes down to it, it is easier to attract existing Christians to the new show in town than to go and make disciples of the unreached.

This phenomenon of the attractional and regional model was evidenced early on when churches moved to the suburbs and created institutions that were detached from place. A neighborhood-focused church that partnered with other local churches within a specific geography to represent Christ to everyone in that area just seemed like plain hard work.

The term "parish" used to hold a lot of meaning. A parish is a specifically defined geographic area in which a church and its people are embedded and where they both live and serve. Today, however, the church has almost entirely lost our understanding of this concept.

At a meeting of foster care agencies in Philadelphia, I (Coz) was approached by one of the leaders of the Catholic services. "I heard your introduction," the man said to me. "You're one of those evangelicals?"

"Yes, I guess you could call me that," I replied.

"Okay, I have a question for you. I've been wondering for a long time why you guys get to choose which church you go to. I mean, how does that work? We just go to the church they tell us to for our neighborhood."

I smiled, but I wondered about the deeper implications of the question. Transportation, technology, culture, economics, and family structure have changed dramatically in the last century, so shouldn't we expect the church to change as well? Why should we care about our local neighborhoods the way churches used to and focus on reaching people there to make disciples in a specific geography?

Because the attractional regional model has failed us miserably in fulfilling the mission given to the church by God to go and make disciples. Because no matter how many large, apparently successful churches we can point to, especially since the introduction of the seeker-sensitive models, overall the church in the United States is in decline. Only in isolation do these growing churches show any kind of success,[4] yet when looked at in the larger picture, not only are they part of a declining church model, they may in fact be a major contributor to that decline.

The missional challenge to us today is that "God wants every man, woman and child to have repeated opportunities to hear, see, be touched by, and respond to an incarnational, geographically close, and linguistically and culturally relevant presentation of the gospel of the Kingdom which proclaims that God in Christ has rectified what the first Adam could not do."[5] For the Philadelphia metropolitan area, that means finding ways to reach out to six million people, of whom Common Grace estimates fewer than one million are currently in a worship entity of any kind on any given Sunday.

Epic is a relatively new church in our city. Just seven years old, it has grown rapidly and now has four locations, with some 1,500 attendees altogether. It uses media technology to transmit the sermon to each location. The church has a young congregation, though in the last few years it has become increasingly multigenerational. Many parents came to see what attracted their children and ended up staying. The church is also quite racially and ethnically diverse. It is indeed a unique gathering.

I (Bill) have been blessed recently to get to know Kent Jacobs, the lead pastor of Epic Church. We've met regularly to engage in discussions about ministry. In a conversation about vision and mission, I challenged him to think about his responsibility to work toward reaching the entire city. After a moment of thought, he said, "We can never do that all by ourselves."

I said, "That's why you need all the partners you can find."

A short time later, a staff member who was aware of the church's desire to be part of reaching all 1.5 million people in the city suggested that Epic could stand for "Every Person in the City." That's it! God wants all 1.5 million people in the city of Philadelphia—and in every city across America and around the world—to hear, see, and be touched by the powerful gospel of Jesus in multiple ways through word and deed ministry.

This vision is far bigger than us, and none of us can fulfill it by ourselves. To achieve this goal, the local church will need to build strategic alliances for the harvest in our local neighborhoods.

This vision changes everything.

2

CALLED TO DISCIPLE MAKING

Christ calls believers to follow Him as disciples. In that work, we carry on His mission of making disciples of the nations through the witness of the gospel. It requires that we be done with the life of sin and follow Christ in a life of whole-souled obedience to all that He has commanded.

Whether we're twenty-five, fifty, or eighty years old, we start out as babies when we come to Christ. At that point, we begin a lifelong process of growing to be like Christ Himself. We will not fully understand spiritual maturity by examining only the lives of the most mature Christians. We must study Christ Jesus Himself. He is the mature One who inspires our growth.

What a contrast discipleship is to our modern concept of church membership! One can be a church member in good standing by merely attending church once or twice a month and contributing modestly to the church treasury. Even after years of regularly attending church, many members today remain babies in Christ. Jesus calls us not to be just church members or attendees but to be His disciples, following Him in His mission to share the gospel with the world.

Indeed, He gives us a high and holy calling to follow Him to make disciples in Matthew 28:19–20.

Go and make disciples of all nations, baptizing them in the name of the Father and of the Son and of the Holy Spirit, and teaching them to obey everything I have commanded you. And surely I am with you always, to the very end of the age.

We will probe these verses around four themes. First, Christ instructs us about the mission of the church. Second, He gives us the message we are to proclaim. Third, He delineates the method. Finally, He will show us the importance of the ministry of the Holy Spirit.

GOD'S MISSION: MAKE DISCIPLES

First, we want to look at God's mission for His church. When we look at Matthew 28:19–20, we find four action words: "go," "make," "baptizing," and "teaching." Only one of these is a command; the other three are participles telling us how to carry out the command. The command, or the mission, in this passage is simply this: "Make disciples!"

In order to make disciples, however, we need to do the other three things. We need to be going, we need to be baptizing, and we need to be teaching the disciples to observe, or obey, all that the Lord has commanded.

The word "disciple" represents a personal attachment between a teacher and a student, a master and a worker. From a Christian point of view, a disciple is a follower of Jesus whose whole life is redirected from sin and self to obedience to Christ.

Jesus said to the disciples, "Go and make disciples of all nations." It is important to understand the concept of the nations if we are to understand our mission. "Nation" comes from the Greek word *ethne*, the origin for our word "ethnic."

When we think of the word "nation," it is natural for us first to think of a geographical or political entity. We are to go to all the nations of the earth, all the different people in different places ruled by different governments. This understanding of geographical nations is reinforced in Acts 2:5: "Now there were staying in Jerusalem God-fearing Jews from every nation." But the word ethne does not just refer to the nations of the world. It is most often used in the New Testament to talk about Gentiles. Now when we use the word "Gentile," we immediately think of a religious distinction between Jews and Gentiles.

In Acts 11:1, we are told that the apostles and brothers in Judea learned the Gentiles had also heard the word of God. The gospel had come at Antioch to the Gentiles, the non-Jewish people. In Ephesians 2:11, the apostle Paul, writing to the Gentile church in Ephesus, speaks of its members as being "called 'uncircumcised' by those who call themselves 'the circumcision.'"

He is clearly referring to Gentiles as "the uncircumcised." The gospel is to go to the uncircumcised—the Gentiles of the world.

But the word ethne also refers even more strongly to the people of the world when it is translated as "heathen" or "pagans." This usage delineates a distinction between believers and unbelievers, between those who are rebels and those who are obedient. Peter says, "Live such good lives among the pagans [ethne] that, though they accuse you of doing wrong, they may see your good deeds and glorify God on the day he visits us" (1 Pet. 2:12). In other words, "Bring the gospel to the pagans." Peter uses ethne again in First Peter 4:3 when he says, "You have spent enough time in the past doing what pagans choose to do—living in debauchery, lust, drunkenness, orgies, carousing and detestable idolatry." Ethne is beginning to sound more like our own world. It's beginning to sound more like our own former ways of life.

Indeed, the origin of ethne in Scripture has to do with the sons of disobedience. We find this most graphically in the Genesis 11 story of the Tower of Babel. As the sons of disobedience there grew in number, they became rebels. They took a stand against the Lord, who had told them to be fruitful, multiply, and fill the earth (see 1:28; 9:1). They were determined not to listen to what God said but instead to stay where they were and make a name for themselves by building a tower up into heaven to show the world how great they were. When the Lord looked down from heaven and saw their rebellion, He decided to confuse their language so that they could no longer conspire together against Him.

This is the beginning of the nations—the different governments, different languages, different ethnic groupings—we know now. From this point on, the story of Scripture is the story of the obedient children of God contrasted with the sons and daughters of disobedience who have chosen to rebel against God. Human history is a long history of the hatred among the peoples of the world—the ethne—and the deep-seated alienation that festers into continual hostility. Christ calls believers to address these walls of alienation with the gospel of Jesus Christ. Only in Christ can and will the walls come down.

What God is saying in His commission to the church is that we are to take the gospel not to believers but to the rebels, the unbelievers. That is the mission. We are to go to the disobedient sinners of the world in the places where they live and raise up a generation of people who are obedient to Jesus Christ. Take the gospel to the Gentiles, the heathens, the pagans, the children of disobedience.

The apostle Paul did just that. When he addressed those gathered together in the Areopagus in Athens, he said:

> People of Athens! I see that in every way you are very religious. For as I walked around and looked carefully at your objects of worship, I even found an altar with this inscription: TO AN UNKNOWN GOD. So you are ignorant of the very thing you worship—and this is what I am going to proclaim to you.

> The God who made the world and everything in it is the Lord of heaven and earth and does not live in temples built by human hands. And he is not served by human hands, as if he needed anything. Rather, he himself gives everyone life and breath and everything else. From one man he made all the nations, that they should inhabit the whole earth; and he

marked out their appointed times in history and the
boundaries of their lands. God did this so that they
would seek him and perhaps reach out for him and
find him, though he is not far from any one of us.
"For in him we live and move and have our being."
As some of your own poets have said, "We are his
offspring." (Acts 17:22–28)

This is why God moves and relocates people to new places—so
they can hear the message of the gospel of Christ. Place matters.

The picture of disobedience is described further in Ephesians
2, where Paul gives a description of our lives before we met Jesus.
This rebellion characterizes the nations to whom God wants us
to carry the gospel.

You were dead in your transgressions and sins, in
which you used to live when you followed the ways
of this world and of the ruler of the kingdom of the
air, the spirit who is now at work in those who are
disobedient. All of us also lived among them at one
time, gratifying the cravings of our flesh and following its desires and thoughts. Like the rest, we were by
nature deserving of wrath. (2:1–3)

Before we met Jesus, we were the ethne. We were among
the children of disobedience—dead sinners under the wrath
and curse of God. Paul goes on to say that in addition to being
dead sinners, we were "Gentiles by birth and . . . separate from
Christ, excluded from citizenship in Israel and foreigners to the
covenants of the promise, without hope and without God in

the world" (Eph. 2:11–12). We didn't know Jesus. We weren't following Jesus. We were excluded from citizenship in Israel, foreigners to the covenants of promise because we were without God in this world.

What a hopeless picture it is to be without Jesus in the world—dead rebels against God without the gospel touching one's life. It is not some distant place Jesus is talking about. He is talking about our own neighborhoods, cities, states, and country. It starts right here.

GOD'S MESSAGE: RECONCILED TO GOD AND EACH OTHER

The message of the gospel is that we can be reconciled to God and therefore to each other. This message of hope is found only in Jesus Christ. In Ephesians 2, Paul tells us that we were dead in our trespasses and sins; but then he says, "Because of his great love for us, God, who is rich in mercy, made us alive with Christ even when we were dead in transgressions—it is by grace you have been saved" (2:4–5). Thank God for the "buts" of Scripture. Yes, we may have a sin dilemma but look at what Jesus has done!

In verses 13–14, after giving us that description of how awful it is to be without Jesus, Paul says, "In Christ Jesus you who once were far away have been brought near by the blood of Christ. For he himself is our peace, who has made the two groups one and has destroyed the barrier, the dividing wall of hostility." In Christ Jesus mercy is to be found!

Not only does Christ make peace for us with God, He makes peace between us and our enemies. When we come to Christ together, we are "no longer foreigners and strangers, but fellow citizens with God's people and also members of his household . . . being built together to become a dwelling in which God lives by his Spirit" (Eph. 2:19–22).

As believers in the Lord Jesus Christ, we are given the assignment of going out into a sin-broken world with the message of God's hope. We are to declare the good news that Jesus has come to set us free from sin and death and bring us into glorious liberty as children of God whose lives will be characterized by obedience to Him. The Lord has given us wonderful insight and made us stewards of the mysteries of His gospel (see 3:6). The Gentiles—the ethne—are heirs together with Israel: members of one family, one household, one body, sharers of the promise in Christ Jesus. Second Corinthians 5 takes it one step further to remind us that we are not just stewards of the mysteries of God, but ambassadors of God and reconciliation:

> Christ's love compels us, because we are convinced that one died for all, and therefore all died. And he died for all, that those who live should no longer live for themselves but for him who died for them and was raised again.

> So from now on we regard no one from a worldly point of view. Though we once regarded Christ in this way, we do so no longer. Therefore, if anyone is in Christ, the new creation has come: The old has gone, the new is here! All this is from God, who reconciled us to himself through Christ and gave us the ministry of reconciliation: that God was reconciling the world to himself in Christ, not counting people's

sins against them. And he has committed to us the message of reconciliation. (2 Cor. 5:14–19)

The Lord has taken us out of darkness, sin brokenness and deadness to bring us into union with Him through Jesus Christ in this thing we call the family of God. Friends with God! Reconciled to God, reconciling with one another. What a glorious ministry the Lord has. We are not engaged in mission impossible. We are engaged in God's great mission. When we are engaged in God's mission, God Himself makes anything possible.

GOD'S METHOD: GOING, BAPTIZING, TEACHING

In our call to be disciples, we should also be disciple makers. When Jesus called Peter, James, and John to leave their fishing nets to follow Him, He also told them, "From now on you will catch men." True disciples always seek to reach and disciple others.

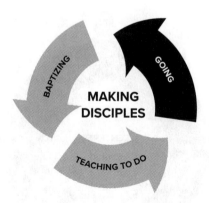

Going. Three concrete actions are necessary to make disciples. The first is to go to the ethne. We will not accomplish the

Lord's mission if we sit at home. The Lord says, "Go! Go to the sin-broken, sin-dead people around you with the glorious gospel of Jesus Christ because that is what the Lord did when He met you." We need not fear disobedient, rebellious people out there because Jesus is able to remold their hearts and lives after His likeness.

All of us have a mission field, sometimes even in our own households. Take a piece of paper and write down the names of the people in your home or extended family who are still strangers to Jesus. They are part of your ethne. Then add to the list the names of your neighbors, even those with whom you may have conflict. They are part of your ethne. Then add your coworkers or your fellow students at school. Not all of us are called to leave our homes and go to distant places; but all of us, as believers in Jesus, are called to share what God has done in our lives with those around us so they can also be introduced to the King of resurrection life. To these we are called to go!

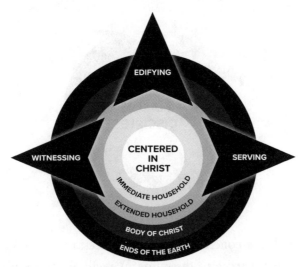

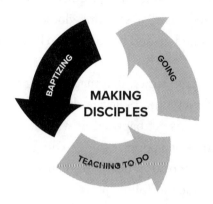

Baptizing. Second, we are called to baptize disciples in the name of the Father, the Son, and the Holy Spirit. The Lord wants us to do more than just tell people about Jesus; He wants us to bring people to Jesus so that they embrace Him. Many people hear and do not believe, but we must continue sharing the gospel until they have embraced Jesus. This is distinctly expressed through baptism.

In Acts 2, when Peter proclaimed the gospel of Jesus Christ on the day of Pentecost, he didn't just sit down after he preached. He urged and pleaded with the people to flee this wicked and perverse generation and embrace Jesus in faith. Without Him, he told them, no life was promised: "Repent and be baptized, every one of you, in the name of Jesus Christ for the forgiveness of your sins" (2:38). That day, three thousand people repented, crossed the line, and said, "I have decided to follow Jesus." They were then baptized (see 2:41).

Baptism lays before us the challenge of being publicly identified with Jesus. In our own day, it is popular to say that a person can be a follower of Jesus in private. You can accept Jesus in the privacy of your own home and the quietness of your own heart. But the Bible tells us that salvation doesn't stop there. It says that we should stand up and be counted to be publicly identified with Jesus.

In New Testament times, that meant going down to the river in full view of everyone. Believers didn't just stand there and watch other believers get baptized. It was the whole town! Getting baptized was not a popular thing to do. People were inviting all the forces of opposition down on themselves by saying publicly, "I have decided to follow Jesus." But Jesus tells us, "Whoever publicly acknowledges me before others, the Son of Man will also acknowledge before the angels of God. But whoever disowns me before others will be disowned before the angels of God" (Luke 12:8–9).

The mission to make disciples is not complete simply by going out and witnessing about Christ. We must work to incorporate those who respond into the local body of believers. The point of entry for people who are new to the faith is baptism. It is there that the believer declares his or her intention to follow Christ.

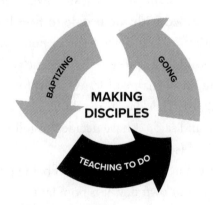

Teaching to obey Christ's commands. The Lord really separates the wheat from the chaff in the third action we are to take as disciple makers. Besides going, besides baptizing people into the body of Christ, we are also called to teach people to observe or obey all that the Lord has commanded.

Obedience goes hand in hand with faith and repentance in Jesus Christ. People come to Jesus so they can be forgiven for their sins but also so they can follow after Him in His life. It means going where He goes, speaking as He speaks, doing as He does. When people turn from sin to Jesus, He says to them, "Come, follow me . . . and I will send you out to fish for people" (Mark 1:17).

The gospel's work is not complete in our lives when we simply embrace Jesus in faith. We must embrace Jesus in faith so that our lives are clearly characterized by obedience to Jesus. He doesn't tell us to go and teach them something *about* Him or His commands. He says that we are to teach them to *do* His commands.

Parents know the difficulties of this challenge. It is one thing for children to know what their parents have asked them to do; it is another thing for them to actually do it. It takes a lot of work to move from giving a command to working obedience into the lives of children so that when they hear a command, they do it. In our work of disciple making, God says that it is not enough to teach people what the commands are, as awesome a task as that is. People must learn to obey the commands that God has given. This is where we separate the infants in the faith from the more mature believers. We like to think the first words babies learn to say will be "Mommy" or "Daddy," but it's usually "no!" Oftentimes believers, when they hear the commands of God, say no!

Our mission to make disciples is not complete until the baptized learns to do the commands of the Lord. Scripture is consistent in insisting on obedience for disciples. In John 14:15 Jesus says, "If you love me, you will keep my commandments" (ESV). In First Peter 1:2, writing to God's elect, Peter says that we "have been chosen according to the foreknowledge of God the Father, through the sanctifying work of the Spirit, to be obedient to Jesus Christ and sprinkled with his blood." John, in First John 2:3, says, "We know that we have come to know him if we keep his commands." Paul writes to the Ephesians, "We are God's handiwork, created in Christ Jesus to do good works, which God prepared in advance for us to do" (Eph. 2:10). Finally, in Hebrews 5:8–9 we read, "Son though he was, he learned obedience from what he suffered and, once made perfect, he became the source of eternal salvation for all who obey him."

Hebrews 5:13–14 sums it up clearly: Anyone who lives on milk, being still an infant, is not acquainted with the teaching about righteousness. But solid food is for the mature, who by constant use have trained themselves to distinguish good from evil.

Disciples are people whose whole lives have turned from sin and are redirected to faith and obedience to Jesus.

THE MINISTRY OF THE HOLY SPIRIT

There is the mission—to make disciples. There is the message—the gospel of Jesus Christ. There is the method—going, baptizing, and teaching to obey. Finally, there is the promise of God Himself living with us. Jesus finishes His Great Commission by saying, "Surely I am with you always, to the very end of the age" (Matt. 28:20). This is the promise of the ministry of the Holy Spirit.

This passage has always caused me to ponder what Jesus meant. Just prior to ascending to heaven, Jesus told His disciples, "Don't be afraid as you go and share the gospel, because I will be with you." Then almost immediately, He rose up into the clouds and was gone, not to return until the Second Coming! What was up? Was that an idle promise? Did He mean the promise or didn't He?

He meant it. But the promise is one to be pondered. John 14–17 helps us with this, because in these chapters Jesus tells us over and over that it is a good thing that He died, rose from the dead, and was going to ascend to heaven because then He would send us His Holy Spirit. Listen to what he says: "The Advocate, the Holy Spirit, whom the Father will send in my name, will teach you all things and will remind you of everything I have said to you" (14:26).

He goes on to teach that the Spirit will testify about Jesus.

> When he comes, he will prove the world to be in the wrong about sin and righteousness and judgment: about sin, because people do not believe in me; about righteousness, because I am going to the Father, where you can see me no longer; and about judgment, because the prince of this world now stands condemned. (16:8–11)

Because Jesus has ascended, the Spirit has come. He leads the way in the disciple-making mission of the church. In John 16, Jesus delineates this spiritual leadership.

> I have much more to say to you, more than you can
> now bear. But when he, the Spirit of truth comes, he
> will guide you into all the truth. He will not speak
> on his own; he will speak only what he hears, and
> he will tell you what is yet to come. He will glorify
> me because it is from me that he will receive what he
> will make known to you. All that belongs to the Fa-
> ther is mine. That is why I said the Spirit will receive
> from me what he will make known to you. (John
> 16:12–15)

Finally, when Paul was in prison, he wrote to the Philippian church to encourage them to keep sharing the gospel of Jesus Christ. It was not a ministry of despair. It was not a mission impossible. It was the intention of God Himself.

> In all my prayers for all of you, I always pray with
> joy because of your partnership in the gospel from
> the first day until now, being confident of this, that
> he who began a good work in you will carry it on
> to completion until the day of Christ Jesus. (Phil.
> 1:4–6)

You see what the Lord was saying? He commits Himself to continue His work in us and through us until we grow up to be like Jesus in obedience. God commits Himself to us until the end. God is not done with us yet. He is continuing the sanctify-ing work of the Spirit in our lives until He brings us to comple-tion, until each and every one of us is like the Savior Himself.

NOT MISSION IMPOSSIBLE

You're probably thinking, every man, woman, and child of the millions (or hundreds or thousands) in our city? Really? Yes, really. It isn't all that great a barrier if each disciple reaches just one new person each year. Dawson Trotman, founder of the Navigators ministry, argued that disciple making is the missing dynamic in much of today's evangelism, which tends to highlight the initial decision of a believer while not engaging in the lifelong ministry of disciple making.[1]

If you were the only believer in Philadelphia today, you could reach and disciple everybody in this place in just twenty-one and a half years. In fact, we could reach and disciple the world's entire population in just thirty-four years if each one of us were to reach and disciple one person each year. It can be done if we will just do the joyful work of making disciples of each and every new believer and teaching them to be disciple makers themselves.

3

THE CHURCH AND THE CITY

In our call to make disciples of all nations, where should we place our pulpits? Where will our ministries have the greatest impact? Too often the church has overlooked, even run from, one of the greatest places in the world for us to place our pulpits—in our own cities.

We all face barriers to sharing the gospel. Rivers with few bridges, major highways, wide streets, and railroad lines divide one community from the next. Some housing communities have walls that isolate one region from another. Racial and ethnic barriers divide us as well; but perhaps the most challenging barrier is created by gang turf, which highlights just how difficult building relationships can be.

The problem: Churches too often step back from these kinds of walls and retreat into isolation and insulation. But Paul tells us in Ephesians 2 that Christ didn't run from walls of alienation and hostility. Instead, He went to the wall of alienation and tore it down in His redemptive work. When He died on the cross, Christ unified broken, divided humanity as one. In doing so, He created one new humanity together of the household of God, built on the foundation of the apostles and prophets, with Christ Jesus as the chief cornerstone.

Today, many would say that we should place our pulpits "in the front of the church sanctuary, of course." But where did Christ and His apostles place their pulpits?

- In the synagogue in Capernaum (Luke 4:31–37)

- At a wedding in Cana of Galilee (John 2:1–11)

- As Jesus traveled and encountered people in their affliction (John 5:1–9)

- In a home where a paralytic was lowered through the roof (Matt. 9:1–8; Luke 5:18–26)

- Along the way when Jesus healed a man who was blind from birth (John 9)

- At a well in Samaria (John 4:1–42)

- In a boat on a turbulent sea (Matt. 8:23–27)

- On a hillside with a multitude of hungry people (John 6:1–13)

- At the grave of Jesus' dear friend Lazarus (John 11:1–44)

- In the garden of Gethsemane (Matt. 26:36–46)

- Before the Sanhedrin (Matt. 26:57–68)

- Before Pilate (Matt. 27:11–26)

- On the cross (Luke 23:32–43)

- Among the believers following the Resurrection (Luke 24:13–49)

Paul was extremely aware of the walls that separated people in his day. The Jews were divided from their Roman occupiers, from the Greeks (particularly by language), and most immediately, from the Gentiles. Where did Paul place his pulpit?

He met Jesus on a road to Damascus, where he was going to persecute believers (see Acts 9:1–8). He had a private meeting with Ananias, who healed his blindness from the light on the road (see 9:10–19). He met with Barnabas, who sought him out upon hearing that he was now a believer (see 9:26–31). He placed his pulpit in a jail cell in Philippi (see 16:16–40), in the Areopagus in Athens (see 17:16–31), and in a synagogue on Cyprus among those who should have believed because of the promises of the covenant (see 13:4–12). Paul stood before the Roman governor, Felix, in Jerusalem (see 24:1–26) and before Agrippa, the king appointed over Israel (see 25:23–26:32).

What do we learn from this survey? That Jesus and His followers placed their pulpits in public spaces, among those who were not yet believers. We should then ask ourselves: What are the implications for our ministries? How does this challenge us?

The gospel is most powerfully demonstrated at the walls of hostility and alienation in the world around us. We see this most pointedly in Christ's atoning, reconciling work on the cross. Like Jesus, we must take notice of people who are broken and in poverty and be willing to go and live alongside them in their need.

LEARNING TO LOVE THE CITY

I (Bill) was born in 1943, the fourth child in the Krispin household, on the north side of Chicago. Two more children came later.

Throughout my childhood we lived in apartments. Our family never had a car, so walking was our main form of transportation if we were going anywhere within three miles of the house. My father worked as a postal clerk and chose to live close to an L train stop convenient to his job. In my early days, our surroundings were alive and vibrant. Everything we needed—grocery store, bakery, five-and-dime store, shoe shop—was within walking distance.

My father often commented on the various neighborhoods we walked through around the city. He knew the history, the churches, the changes. He had lived most of his life from early childhood in the city, and he didn't want to live anywhere else. He often said that a person could raise his children in the city when the Lord was in the house. I didn't realize it at the time, but I inherited my love of the city from my father. Though his commentary about it bored me as a child, I learned to love how cities are places of continual, dynamic change.

Most churches in those days were neighborhood churches with small congregations. Many bore the neighborhood name and almost everyone was able to walk to service. In my early years, however, our family went to a church some distance from home. We had to take two buses to get there. But as my siblings and I entered our teenage years, our parents decided to attend a church within walking distance so that we could be involved in youth activities. In its early years, that church was very much a neighborhood church.

The years 1953–1960 turned Chicago upside down. During the Eisenhower years, America's interstate highway system was built; and in a relatively brief time, five major expressways were carved into the neighborhoods of the city. Tens of thousands of households were displaced to make way for them. In that short period, the available housing stock of Chicago was decimated.

Few relocation services were available for those displaced, our family included. Because there were so many of us, it was difficult for my parents to find us another place to live. As a result, we were the last family living in a large apartment building as the neighborhood around us was slowly torn down to make space for the road. For two years, my parents searched for another place to live. They finally found an apartment nearby; but, unfortunately, the realtor they used hadn't been up-front with the new landlord that five children would be living there. Our new rent was already forty dollars higher than at our previous place; and when he found out about the size of our family, he immediately raised it another twenty dollars. That new apartment never felt like home for us, even though we lived there throughout the remainder of our childhood.

Throughout all this, the church did not respond with any help in meeting our family crisis. That deeply impacted me. Although I continued to attend church, I wandered away from the Lord over time.

A vast percentage of those needing to relocate made their way to the suburbs; and once the expressways opened, that trend accelerated. Because of this migration, Chicago's population dropped by 1.5 million over the next decades. Urban neighborhoods were decimated and robbed of their holistic cohesiveness. Homes were lost, as were hundreds of businesses. Shopping districts went dead in a short period of time.

Slowly, the neighborhood churches became commuter churches. By my late teens, our family was one of only a few in our congregation who still lived in the neighborhood. Eventually, our church planted a daughter church in a nearby suburb in order to provide a locale for the members who now lived there. The congregation that remained in the city was an ethnic congregation of Norwegian immigrants. Each Sunday, we had services in Norwegian for the older generation and recent immigrants, and an English service for the younger generations.

The church maintained a mission home to house male heads of households who had preceded their families in coming to America. Gradually immigration dried up, and the home became a residence for single men and women. As families moved out of our area, new families moved in. First poor whites came, but eventually the rapidly growing Latino population began to move in. This led our congregation to start a Spanish-language service. The Norwegian service finally ended, but our congregation remained bilingual.

This story was not restricted to our church. It was repeated again and again by most of the surrounding churches. From my youthful perspective, the church was leaving the city and it sure seemed like God was leaving too. My anger toward the church grew as I saw it close its heart to the city. But after my conversion, all of this converged to shape my call to ministry in the city.

I attended North Park University on the north side of Chicago as a commuter student who worked full time. After college, I went on to attend seminary at Westminster Theological Seminary just outside of Philadelphia. During my first year, however, I found living in a suburb to be isolating and boring; so in my second year, I was offered an internship at the Tenth Presbyterian Church in downtown Philadelphia. The pastor, Dr. Mariano DiGangi, knew of my interest in urban ministry and assigned me to serve part of my time at the Evangel Presbyterian Church in south Philly, an urban congregation in its final days of life. Once a vibrant church, it was down to a small remnant.

The doors of the church were kept open by Miss Hannah, an elderly woman who had an enormous heart for the young people of the community and single-handedly carried on a large youth ministry. She had remarkable control of the place, even though a couple hundred youth often attended. She even refereed basketball games in the gym while wearing high-heeled shoes. She knew nothing about basketball, so she set her own rules for the games: no hitting and no tripping. Miss Hannah assigned foul shots based on her perception of the severity of the offense. She mentored me in my sense of calling and placement and became a significant influence in my life. At the end of the year, she asked me to consider moving into the community to start a new church. She said she could let her church close if I would start a new one. That conversation began for me what would become more than fifty years of ministry in Philadelphia.

But remember, I was thinking that God had left the city. My experience with Miss Hannah's church only reinforced that notion—until I met Brother Willard. After that internship year, my wife and I moved into that community in south Philly. We purchased a home that would serve as both our residence and a ministry base for developing the new church. We spent our initial time in the house doing renovations. One day, while working at the house, I heard a knock at the door. When I opened it, I looked up—way up—at a man who seemed about eight feet tall (I found out later that he was six foot eight). Without introducing himself he asked me, "Why are you here?"

Flustered, I struggled with how to respond but eventually managed to say, "I am here as an ambassador of Christ to plant a church."

Without hesitation he then asked, "Are you going to do like all the other white folks, pretending that God doesn't have any people in the black church?" He had me there. Until he asked that, that is what I had been doing.

He introduced himself as Brother Willard and told me he was a Baptist minister living on the next block. He had an itinerant ministry that helped black churches establish community Sunday schools. I was speechless, thinking he wanted me to pack my bags and go back to where I had come from. Instead he told me, "If you will, come with me and I'll introduce you to what God is doing through His people in the black community."

Over the next months, Brother Willard took me to various places, one of which was a 6 a.m. prayer group of pastors who met at the Manna Bible Institute, then located in west Philly. That prayer group became the place where I was discipled for urban ministry. In my first summer with them, the group was burdened for the street youth of Philadelphia, especially as the city faced a long teachers' strike. Their prayers rapidly became plans to start a Christian school for street youth in north Philadelphia. Their timeline was just three weeks.

I wasn't prepared for what followed. I was the only person in the prayer group who was full time in ministry. Consequently, I became the feet for the project. Remarkably, the school did open in three weeks and the prayer group became its board. The rest is history. The same group then established the Center for Urban Theological Studies (CUTS), where I served for the next twenty-seven years. In a very short period of time, I was turned upside down, shaken up, and redirected through that group of faithful brothers. One year became more than fifty years of service in the church in Philadelphia. To God be the glory for the great things He has done and is doing!

FOLLOWING THE CITY'S CHANGES

A few years ago, Common Grace was commissioned to help with community studies for a group of Latino faith-based non-profits. We were quite surprised when we received the list of these ministries and saw their addresses. One nonprofit was in the north Philly community of Hunting Park, where my wife and I lived, but the others? Smaller cities well outside of Philadelphia: Reading, Bethlehem, Allentown, Bristol, and Lancaster. We had known that the Latino population had been moving toward northeast Philly; but this was a completely different set of cities, most of them with under one hundred thousand people and most based around a single industry or serving a rural area. What was causing this movement?

As we began our work, the surprises continued. The indicators of poverty in all of those smaller cities were at similar levels to those we saw in major cities: lack of quality education, disproportionate allocation of county resources, high crime, open drug dealing. What stood out the most, however, is where the families in those communities had come from—most from New York City, followed by Philadelphia and places like Trenton and Camden. Families had been moving from major urban centers to these smaller cities. Our quest to understand the movement began after we knew the data.

Soon after this, I (Coz) took a group of students biking in New York City. I love to bike and have ridden in many places, both urban and rural. I try to ride in New York at least once a year, parking my car on Staten Island and catching the ferry into Manhattan.

I have a little history with New York City. Back in 1992, I arrived in New York from England, where I had been working and traveling. Well, actually I arrived in Newark, New Jersey and thought that "Newark" was just how Americans pronounced "New York." I couldn't understand why people at the transit terminal kept telling me I needed to catch a bus under the river to the city. You can all laugh.

My accommodations were up around 102nd and Amsterdam, quite a different place back then than it is now. It was a pretty ugly area. New York in general was quite the shock to me. Before I made my requisite visit to Times Square, all my roommates told me stories of being robbed somewhere around that area. I had traveled a lot and been to some of the largest cities in the world, but urban America was different. People had warned me not to go to Belfast in the 1990s because of the IRA issues, but I found it to be one of the most welcoming places I have ever traveled. Istanbul was another place I had been warned away from because of the Kurds blowing up bridges; but again, I had no problems there. Serbia right after its war broke out, Greece during its rolling strikes (which still seem to be going on more than twenty years later)—the list could go on with places others said were not safe that all received this Aussie very well. No offense, but New York City was the first city I was ever scared in.

While it's true that in New York I fell in love with cities and the work God was doing through amazing men and women like Bo Nixon, Alex Wright, the Westbrooks (okay, so they are in Newark, but it still sounds the same to me), much of early 90s Manhattan was rough.

On our bike trip through New York City on this particular day, we took the subway into the lower Bronx and biked toward Chinatown. Dodging cabs and swerving around buses kept us sharp, but generally speaking, it was easy pedaling. As our group biked, however, I noticed something: The city had changed dramatically since I lived there. The new urbanites had come into much of New York. For many people, it was a much better place: It boasted cool cafés, bike lanes, microbreweries, safer streets, and renewed housing development. The same dynamic was happening in much of Boston, Philly, and Washington, DC. Gentrification had arrived.

That day, I wondered where all the people who used to live there had gone. National numbers continued to show that the gap between the rich and the poor was growing, not shrinking. Poverty hadn't been addressed in those parts of New York City; it had just moved into smaller cities. Large numbers of people from Manhattan, Harlem, the Bronx, and Brooklyn now resided in Reading, Pennsylvania, which in 2014 was the poorest city in America. DC had similarly and effectively pushed the poor into

Prince George's County, Maryland. Boston and Philly had also moved the poor from the urban centers once abandoned by the white community who now wanted them back.

UNDERSTANDING AND ADAPTING

Sadly, tragically, the church has been complicit in both white flight and gentrification, both at the expense of the urban poor, both with little regard for the poor. People can argue all day that the new wave of churches reaching the gentrifiers and hipsters are socially conscious and have all kinds of mercy ministries; but very few of these churches have members from the remaining poorer urban communities, and almost never anyone in leadership from those communities. This isn't simply a racial issue (although it is in part). It's an economic issue and another strong example that few churches understand the complexities and the people within their local communities.

People moving from the cities to the suburbs are being replaced at an even more rapid rate by people moving into the cities, particularly suburban "relocaters" or new immigrants. Dynamic change is taking place all across the United States as people move from one community to the next. But few churches really understand these changes and when they do, they often cannot adapt to them. If we hope to reach our communities with the good news of the gospel and make disciples of men, women, and children, we must become aware of what is happening in our areas and be willing to go to and identify with the people around us in their need.

4

BREAKING DOWN WALLS OF DIVERSITY

Since urban change is a reality in our nation (and increasingly around the world), we need to understand this movement if we, as God's people, are going to make disciples. And once we begin to understand it, we need to take action. This can be difficult, especially when the people around us seem different from us, whether by age, race, economic status, or otherwise, but Christ has shown us how to break down walls between diverse people groups and create a beautiful oneness between them.

Philadelphia has not been as quick as New York City to gentrify, but its suburbanization has been one of the most rapid in the United States. It offers a stark picture of the realities involved in the cultural and racial shifts taking place in many of our communities.

THE CHANGING CITY OF PHILADELPHIA

Philadelphia is a complex urban center surrounded by a still-growing metropolitan region. It has a long and detailed history, leading the nation in both positive and negative ways. Philadelphia was designed to be the new utopia, an open city, by its founder, William Penn. Yet even Penn himself chose not to live in the city proper, instead residing on his country estate some twenty miles northeast of the city. Philadelphia is a city of neighborhoods, with more than four hundred officially on record and hundreds more known to local residents. Its population is just over 1.5 million, but the metropolitan region has about 6 million residents.

Philadelphia has grown steadily since its inception, consuming outlying townships into the city and establishing the current city limits in 1854. By the 1920s, Philadelphia had a population of around 2 million people, which held steady for thirty years, then began a decline. Between 1980 and 1990, Philadelphia's population fell by 500,000, falling below 1.4 million and leading the nation in the move from urban to suburban living.

Many factors led to that decline. The construction of the interstate road system created rapid access from the suburbs into the city. The GI Bill encouraged the pursuit of the American dream of single-family, disconnected housing. White flight took place, as white people did not want to live in communities where African Americans were migrating and instead created their own new communities outside the city.

Family size declined as well. In 1960, the average family had 3.67 people but by 2015, that number had dropped to 3.14. More important, the shape of families in the city changed radically. In 1960, 73 percent of all families consisted of two parents with children. Only 9 percent were single-parent families and another 14 percent were two-parent families through remarriage. By 2014, the percentages had changed radically.

Only 46 percent were families consisting of two parents in a first-time marriage together with their children. Another 15 percent were two-parent families through remarriage, another 7 percent were two-parent cohabiting families, and 26 percent were single-parent families. Traditional families no longer prevailed in the city. That reality had huge implications for the church, which historically has focused ministry on two-parent families with little ministry to families impacted by divorce.

Although the city was losing vast numbers of people, the growth in the suburbs outpaced those losses. The net loss of population in Philadelphia was 500,000, but the gross loss was far higher because African Americans were migrating from southern states and immigrants were arriving in Philadelphia and replenishing the numbers of those leaving. It is likely that close to 750,000 Philadelphians moved to the suburbs, in that short period of time.

One of the first institutions to leave a declining community is the church and Philadelphia saw that happen in abundance. Some churches chose to follow their congregants as they moved, others closed down, and some attempted to change in an effort to meet the new community's needs. While this took place, new church plants began in the suburbs. The conversation among many denominations, especially white ones, was that the future of the church was in the suburbs, and they missed the changing opportunities in the city.

In some cities, like Boston, the black and ethnic minority churches saw and understood this change well. The riots of the 1960s seemed to spark an earlier white flight in Boston; and by the early 1970s, the church in the city was almost dead, with an estimated less than 3 percent of the population attending church on any given Sunday. Into this void stepped the black, Latino, and immigrant churches, perhaps feeling that they were finally free to work without restraint. They sparked what is known in Boston as the "quiet revival,"[1] which led to not only an almost doubling in the number of churches but also a growth of attendance from 3 percent to almost 15 percent. This was a remarkable achievement and an affirmation that the city wasn't a wasteland to flee but rather a place of great spiritual awakening and opportunity. Philadelphia did not experience the same incredible resurgence, although the black and Latino churches did grow.

In the suburbs, built for families that owned and used cars, the entire dynamic of community was different. Most suburbs were not built for walking, lacked public transit, and allowed people to live separated lives. Shopping was done in specific areas, early on in strip malls and then later in larger shopping malls.

But as more people occupied the suburbs, the road systems back into the cities became increasingly clogged due to workers commuting, so businesses began constructing their office buildings and manufacturing in the suburbs. This eventually led to edge cities, communities on the edge of major cities that functioned as their own cities. In the Philadelphia region, places like Conshohocken and Norristown were early edge cities, and ones like King of Prussia are still growing into that role. The suburbs were, in effect, beginning to urbanize.

That continues today with malls being built as outdoor spaces or with new town-center-style construction. Public transportation increased in the suburbs and the suburban sprawl slowed. This was certainly due in part to the poor state of the roads and people no longer willing to spend as much time commuting. It was also part of a changing trend of younger people wanting to live lives different from those of their parents. Essentially, the suburbs are urbanizing and the cities are suburbanizing.

In cities like Philadelphia, we have now seen black flight and even Latino flight, following a similar trend as that of white flight in the 1980s. Meanwhile, the children of the white flight generation are returning to the cities. All this has created rapid and dynamic change. Following the huge population declines and stagnation through the 1980s and 1990s, Philadelphia is once more a growing city in a growing state, with much of the growth coming from Latino and Asian immigration. Waves of young people, almost all white, are moving into the city's inner neighborhoods—Northern Liberties, Fairmount, Brewerytown, Fishtown, Passyunk, Bella Vista, and Center City South. Older retirees are also coming back to the city, both white and black, rebuilding formerly dilapidated communities in south and west Philadelphia. The University of Pennsylvania and its neighboring higher education institutes, as well as Temple University, have created their own communities with policing and urban-development priorities. Philadelphia's baseball and football teams sell out their stadiums with tens of thousands of people coming into the city. The city's hospitals and universities are cited among the best in the nation, with a reported one in six doctors in America having completed some of their training in the Philadelphia area.

To many people, especially those who live outside the city limits, Philadelphia provides all they could want in a metropolitan capital: great higher education, dedicated medical professionals, winning sports teams, modern and historical arts, the most urban parkland in America, and all these things available along a road system designed for the suburbanite to access the best of Philadelphia without ever encountering the difficulties the city faces.

With an estimated 2,500 churches, Philadelphia has a rich church history dating back to the founding of the city. According to Ram Cnaan at the University of Pennsylvania, these churches each contribute almost half a million dollars annually to the welfare of the community in direct and indirect services.[2] Many denominations and parachurch mission agencies either began in Philadelphia or have had their home in the city. The African Methodist Episcopal (AME) Church, the first black American denomination, began in Philadelphia, and the city's churches were pivotal in working toward ending slavery as well as in the civil rights movement. Well-known seminaries and Christian colleges came from Philadelphia, including Conwell Seminary, Westminster Seminary, Palmer Seminary, Biblical Seminary, Reformed Episcopal Seminary, Saint Charles Borromeo Seminary, Lutheran Seminary, Cairn University, Eastern University, LaSalle University, and Villanova University, among others.

The problems the city faces, however, are many and incredibly complex. Philadelphia's public schools are a disaster, with a graduation rate below 50 percent for black and Latino males, reportedly the lowest in the nation. Last year, there were more than 4,500 reported assaults in the schools and hundreds more that were not reported. Some schools have become so terrible that the school board has been handing them over to charter schools in the hopes that they can do something where the public schools have been failing so miserably. This is only the beginning of the city's complex issues. Philadelphia has more than eight thousand children under the care of the Department of Human Services (DHS). Forty-two percent of children in Philadelphia who enter DHS's care and are reunified with their families reenter DHS care within twelve months. Approximately 660 children are waiting for immediate adoption in Philadelphia. These adoptions are free and the adoptive parents receive a substantial monthly stipend and complimentary medical services for the child until he or she reaches the age of eighteen. DHS workers say the 660 number does not even represent the true problem. There are hundreds more children that workers don't bother to put up for adoption, believing there is no real point to it. This issue becomes even more complex when we consider that DHS's $550 million budget comes mostly from state and federal governments on a matching ratio of ten to one—in other words, for every dollar the city spends on child welfare, the state and federal governments give them ten dollars. This creates a classic problem in which reducing the city's spending by a dollar means the city loses ten dollars in state and federal funding. Incentives to change the current state of child welfare in Philadelphia are majorly hindered by such a system.

Philadelphia averages almost one homicide a day and the majority of the victims are young black males. In the 19124 zip code where I (Coz) live, more than six hundred prisoners are released into the community each year at a cost of $58 million. The majority of these prisoners are released into an area of Frankford I like to call the "Twilight Zone," which was created by a historical deed restriction made in the 1930s on one side and the building of an elevated transit line on the other. Large homes became ideal for illegal halfway houses and drug rehabs, easy access to the El led to increased drug trafficking, and home ownership fell to 25 percent compared to 75 percent in surrounding communities.

Philadelphia has been marred by public corruption for as long as anyone can remember. The mayor from 2000–2008, John Street, had no problem speaking publicly of his policy of "pay to play," giving city contracts to those who contributed to his campaigns. Numerous city council members, state representatives, and city government workers have been indicted on corruption charges. Yet Philadelphians are either accepting of these systems or just feel helpless. Back in 1903, reporter Lincoln Steffens made a statement that seems to ring true today: Philadelphia is "no more corrupt than any other major American city, but what sets it apart is that people seem content with that corruption."[3]

It is safe to say that Philadelphia has significant challenges and real assets. The city cannot be defined by its problems or its strengths but is a complex conglomeration of both these things. This is to be expected in a city this old and this large.

Likewise, the state of the church in Philadelphia cannot be told in simple terms. The city has lost dozens, if not hundreds, of churches over the past fifty years. Mainline denominations such as the Presbyterian Church of the United States of America, the Methodist Church, and the Lutheran Church have closed many of their buildings. Much of this is due to their congregants leaving the communities and the churches not understanding or willing to adapt to the new people arriving in their areas. Some congregations have relocated to where their parishioners now live, but many more have ceased to exist.

At the same time, there has been a rise in the number of small churches, often called "storefronts," as well as growth in the black Pentecostal church (some independent, some part of denominations). Has the number of new churches kept pace with the number closing down? Without a comprehensive study it is difficult to say, but the influence of the church on local communities may have declined. Common Grace has stated that the church is in decline, believing that less than 10 percent of Philadelphia's population is in church on any given Sunday and the average life span of a church is falling dramatically.

The trending of the black population to the suburbs has also given rise to a far more suburbanized black church. A growing number of black churches are found in Philadelphia's suburbs and most of the larger black churches located in the city have commuting congregations, many of whose members, especially their leadership, now live in the suburbs.

BREAKING DOWN WALLS

To illustrate the full implications of the gospel and its power to break down walls, Paul drew on the design of the Jerusalem temple in Ephesians 2, showing us the Lord's preferred way to express the power of the gospel to the world—the cross. Through it, Christ addressed the deepest and most profound alienation, hostility, and brokenness in the world and brought about reconciliation between man and God and various groups.

The Temple was the place where God dwelt with His people. But though God lived among His people, they did not have free and open access to His presence, because sin created a barrier between God and man. This was illustrated in the walls of alienation that divided the Temple.

First, God was alienated from humankind, as shown by the veil of the inner temple in front of the Holy of Holies.

Interior Design of Jerusalem's Temple[4]

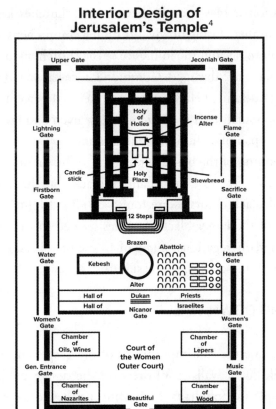

The Holy Place was separated from the multitudes of Israel. While the Jewish people were near God, they had access to Him only through the work of the high priest on the Day of Atonement. Consequently, they were still outside the Holy of Holies where God dwelt. There was also a separate section in the temple court to divide men and women. Finally, a wall separated Jews from Gentiles (the "far off," Acts 2:39). Gentiles, the unclean that Jews were not even to touch, did not have any access into the Holy of Holies. Paul illustrates in Ephesians 2:11–12 how deeply divided and alienated the Gentiles were from the Jews. The Gentiles were "in the flesh" (ESV) by virtue of their uncircumcision—separated from Christ, alienated from the commonwealth of Israel, strangers to the covenants of promise, having no hope without God in the world. But Christ, in His atoning and reconciling work, broke down these walls. Jews and Gentiles were both sinners for whom Jesus died. He didn't save them separately but died in their place at the cross. In so doing, Christ reconciled both groups to God by tearing down the veil of the temple and opening access to the presence of God with His atoning sacrifice. The result? One new humanity.

Gentiles were no longer strangers and aliens to God or to Jews. Now both Jews and Gentiles were members together in the family of God. All of them became the place where God dwelled (the temple of God's presence). At the cross and with the resurrection, God moved out of Jerusalem to live in and among His people. This new community was now built on the foundation of the apostles and prophets, with Christ as the chief cornerstone.

GOING WHERE THE NEED EXISTS

Where are the walls of alienation in our communities? We can find them among many individuals and groups:

- Members of broken families

- People addicted to drugs and alcohol

- Those incarcerated, as well as their families struggling outside the prison walls

- Racial groups—blacks, whites, Latinos, Asians, others

- Biracial families (almost always alienated from churches that are monocultural so that neither spouse is comfortable)

- Language groups (first-generation immigrants often never develop fluency in English, which also creates a chasm between parents and children)

- Rich and poor

- Those who have differing levels of education

- Police, who frequently have hostile relationships with communities

First Baptist Church in Flushing, New York is a great example of a church facilitating God's reconciliation between people and God, and between dissimilar groups of people. It has a multiethnic, multicultural ministry in one of the most diverse communities in the country. Each Sunday, it has four worship services in a modest-sized building. One service is in English, focused on second and third generations of immigrant families; another is in Spanish; and two are in Mandarin, one a traditional service and the other more contemporary for the young Chinese generation. First Baptist, led by senior pastor Rev. Henry Kwan, sees itself as one church with many faces.

We should reach out to those in need of drug and alcohol recovery and rehabilitation. This is often too big for just one congregation to handle, but working in partnership with others in the community can be effective in making this type of ministry available.

We need to create educational access for the disenfranchised. In Boston, the Emmanuel Gospel Center has a ministry arm focused on creating a successful path from high school through college for at-risk urban young people. The Boston Education Collaborative (BEC) has helped dozens of churches engage effectively in this ministry. They have been doing this for over twenty years, and the churches have had a significant impact on the youth they have served.

We need to advocate for widows, single parents, and their children, putting those who are alone into the family of God: "A father to the fatherless, a defender of widows, / is God in his holy dwelling. / God sets the lonely in families, / he leads out the prisoners with singing" (Ps. 68:5–6).

We need effective urban churches to raise up and embrace diverse leadership teams from our communities.

As people called to make disciples in our communities, we need to welcome everyone around us, not just those who are like us. Christ can effect reconciliation between people and God, as well as between diverse groups of people.

5

WHERE ARE WE SPENDING OUR RESOURCES?

The economic structure and resourcing in a church can strongly influence how that church interacts with its local community. It can also be a great indicator of the focus of our ministries. As the common saying goes, "If you want to know how something works, follow the money!" The question for us is: Where is our focus? Is it on the people who actually live in our communities? Or are we, perhaps unknowingly, spending our time and money on our own needs?

People have many strategies around church planting, from low-cost bivocational efforts to pouring in significant resources, often hundreds of thousands of dollars, in the initial years. Both can be successful in reaching people, although the expensive plants by nature often end up being more attractional, especially in poorer communities.

Common Grace's small studies have shown that in poorer communities in Philadelphia, churches can expect about $1,000 in giving per member annually, so a seventy-five-member church can expect around $75,000 in financial giving. This is a rough estimate, but we have found it to be reasonably consistent. At that level, and based on the fact that the rate of giving usually lags behind attendance in the early years of church planting, it is difficult for a congregation targeting new converts to grow at a rate that could sustain a high-salaried church plant long term. Many places support new church plants for only three to five years; so if a plant's goal is new conversion growth rather than transfer growth, either the support model or the salary model needs to change. This is just the beginning of the fiscal challenges inherent in today's church models.

WHERE ARE WE SPENDING OUR TIME AND MONEY?

In the early weeks and years of a new church plant, the majority of the leadership's time and resources go to reaching new people for the church. That can take as much as 90 percent of a pastor's time. But as the church grows, leadership usually spends more and more time with those now attending rather than those who don't attend. A great deal of effort goes into the function of the church—Sunday services, running small groups, building a church building, and creating a staff, for example. It is in this crucial stage that most churches begin spending most of their resources on themselves rather than on those who are not yet engaged in the congregation. That might seem like a logical transition for a pastor who is beginning to shepherd a new flock, but the movement from 90 percent outward focus to even 50 percent is in reality a massive switch in resources and it can impact the church for generations to come. The skills required to move from leading an outward-focused team to a team balanced between outward and inward focus are amply covered by others in training conferences and books. Those skills are often used by new business start-ups, as there is such a huge change in the allocation of time and resources during these transitions. This allows them to maintain the balance of outreach and product delivery. The church, however, often finds it difficult to maintain that kind of balance.

Common Grace has analyzed budgets for churches looking to better engage their communities, and we have found that they have often allocated few resources for people not yet involved in the church. Most have a missions budget, usually around 10 percent of their total giving, and the majority of that goes outside their community. Beyond that, the majority of funds tend to be spent on pastoral staff and rent or mortgage for the church building. The argument is often made that the staff is there to teach and train the congregation to do the outreach and disciple making. What tends to happen, though, is that the church focus remains inward, where the money and resources flow. There are always exceptions to this, thankfully, and models like house churches that minimize these effects; but, in general, most churches spend the greatest portion of their money on themselves, not unlike most social clubs.

Worship style, building style, staffing style, parking, decor, and other elements often bring about transfer growth, much like in the entertainment industry. But transfer growth and disciple making are not the same thing. If we think through when and why most people come to Christ, it generally takes place through relationships and times of difficulty. Disciple making, by its very definition, is a relational activity, not an attractional industry. If we are committed to reaching entire communities, we must be focused on the people in those communities. That does not mean a pastor should neglect the flock but rather should teach, train and lead the people to build relationships in their daily lives, creating ripples in the pond.

A great exercise for any church to do, in order to identify where its focus truly lies, is to map out its congregation using different colors to designate four groups: leaders, involved members, attenders, and visitors. This can give the church a good picture of where its people come from and reveal patterns and key points of influence. If the church then overlays its budget on the map, it will most likely find that the budget and the map go hand in hand. The church resources likely flow to those who hold the most influence. Ministries, staffing, and events tend to reflect those holding power in the church. This isn't necessarily a problem unless a church finds that the people receiving money do not live or have a strong presence in the local community. In that case, it will be very difficult for the church to make disciples in its area. There are many reasons that a church's senior pastor may not live in the local community, some of them understandable. But if the majority of a church's leaders do not live in that community, the road to community transformation is almost impossible.

WHOSE RESOURCES ARE THEY?

Many will make the argument that the key people in the church provide a significant amount of the church's funding, so naturally those people should be influential in deciding how that money is spent. But this attitude reveals an inherent problem in the model many churches use because it resembles a social club structure, not the Kingdom.

When someone gives, they give to the Kingdom, to Christ, to His church, and that gift should not be used as a way of influencing policy or direction. That is, of course, an American (and global) way of thinking, so it's not unexpected, but leaders need the courage and faith to defy it. If people withhold their offerings as a way of trying to influence decisions, leaders need to trust that God will bring the resources needed; and the people withholding their gifts need to understand that they are withholding from God, not their own clubs. These are not easy things to address and we are not trying to trivialize the matter, but church leaders often act in fear of losing resources that should not be seen as theirs to lose in the first place.

DOES OUR SPENDING REFLECT OUR COMMUNITIES?

In evaluating where the focus of our ministry lies, another matter to consider is whether the church budget reflects the community in the way it is spent. That brings into sharp focus how a church relates to its community, especially one in transition. When a church is located in a transitioning community, whether that community is changing ethnically, economically, or in age, that church needs to reflect those changes in its culture.

As churches grow and mature, their members often continue to reflect the age and ethnicity of those who first began the church. Most have pastors who are of the same ethnicity and culture as the majority of the church attendees, even if that does not reflect the community around them. What also happens is that most churches expend their resources in a way that reflects the majority culture in the church on a Sunday, not necessarily the majority culture of the community around them.

This makes it difficult for the church to connect with the local community. The way people dress, the music selections, the length of a service, the decor in a building, the times for gathering, the language and printed materials are often reflective of the majority culture inside a church or those in power positions. These types of expressions in a church can either help or hinder. They usually have no scriptural basis but instead are cultural interpretations, which is fine unless they become barriers to interacting with the community.

Visiting a start-up church in Boston, I (Coz) was given a fairly large handout containing the liturgy for that Sunday. It required a lot of reading and following throughout the service in English. It was no surprise that the majority of the people I spoke with after the service were highly educated academics and enjoyed the liturgical style of worship. The leadership, however, spoke of wanting a more diverse gathering, especially including those less formally educated and those who had less economically. I shared with them that their handout could be a barrier, as literacy and economic challenges are often tied together, and handing someone so much to read on first entering the room could be enough to cause that person not to return. It wasn't an easy challenge for the church to overcome, but many liturgical churches have found effective ways to be inclusive of the less literate. The leadership had not seen the challenge at first because neither its congregation nor its friends who came from similar cultural backgrounds struggled with reading English at a high level.

Another cultural group we should seek to reflect is the youth. We at Common Grace do not fully understand current youth culture and by the time we do, it will probably have changed. But we do understand that youth know their own culture and if we want to engage them, the church needs youth at the table to help drive relevance in decision making. Whether we like their culture or not isn't the real issue. The question is: How do we engage their culture and how do we help them engage their culture for the Kingdom? How do we equip them to make disciples?

The church must also relate to second-generation Americans. Reports and studies show the decline of the church among white Americans. Whether this indicates a decline in Christ followers is debatable, but church attendance is markedly down. Is this surprising when the place where people are asked to gather is so culturally disconnected from the culture in which they live? This is particularly noticeable in second-generation immigrant communities, where young people speak English all day to their friends, then sit in church services delivered in a language that their parents speak fluently but children don't fully understand. Many of our great Christian fathers fought to ensure that the Bible was in the language of the people and we celebrate groups like Wycliffe for continuing that work. Why wouldn't we want the same in our own congregations? A church located in a transitioning community should reflect its community's changes. This is not to say that we should compromise our core faith beliefs; rather, we should understand what is *cultural* and what is *Christ*.

We won't go too much into this delicate dance here except to say that if the people in a community are not beginning to come to a church, then the church should be asking difficult questions about itself. If our neighbors don't come to our barbecues, why not? Could it be that our neighbors are Muslim and all we serve is pork sausage? Could it be that our neighbors are young and all we play is fifties music? Could it be that our neighbors have young children and our yards aren't child friendly? Could it be that our neighbors are older and we don't have any comfortable chairs? Or could it be that our neighbors don't even know they are invited?

SELF-EXAMINATION

In north Philadelphia, Epiphany Fellowship acquired a vacant lot right next to the church. Epiphany is a growing church with young adults and many people coming from outside its community. On Sundays, parking is a significant issue for the church and the new lot could have certainly helped in this area. But leaders at Epiphany decided to build a children's playground there, not because they had a lot of young children at the church but because the community had a lot of young children and few playgrounds. Leaders recognized that they needed to expend resources on those they wanted to reach, not those already coming.

This strategy is also reflected in how Epiphany shapes disciple making, who it hires, and how it develops its budget. Its staff and members, no matter where they live, are encouraged to understand and interact with the community around the church, eat at the local restaurants, get to know the neighbors, listen to and learn from them. Building a parking lot, or even refurbishing Sunday school classrooms, took second place to engaging the community in its place of need and listening to its voice. That is courageous leadership.

If we are serious about making disciples of our local communities, transforming our neighborhoods, and seeing new people come to Christ, we need to examine our churches' budgets, leadership, and decision-making structures. Where we put our resources reveals our focus—and whether or not we are effectively following God's call to live the gospel in our communities.

PART 2

THE MEANS—KNOWING OUR COMMUNITIES

6

KNOWING OUR COMMUNITIES' BOUNDARIES

Place matters. But in order to effectively plant churches and make disciples, we need to know the places where we live. This begins by determining the boundaries of our communities.

By boundaries, we do not only mean lines on a map. We do consider the physical boundaries that define a community, but we also take into account the psychological and spiritual boundaries that accompany them. When we meet church leaders or planters for the first time, we ask them how they define their communities' boundaries. The vast majority of the time, they tell us something like, "We look at a five-mile circle around the church building" or "Our church is in such and such zip code and we use that as our boundary." In a suburban or rural context, we are more likely to hear, "We are in Bristol Township" or "We work in Hatfield Borough."

But having visited dozens of cities around the world, we have found that communities aren't formed in circles. Drawing a circle around a church building and calling that its boundary is an ineffective method of defining where our place is. In some communities, zip codes may define a boundary; but in cities like Philadelphia, about the only people that works for are mail carriers. What we ultimately look for as we seek to define boundaries is how people function in real life. In other words, who are the people we are most likely to cross paths with in the areas where we live and why?

A physical boundary can be a major road, the classic train tracks, a creek, the placement of public transit, or government decisions such as the location of public housing; but other types of boundaries can be defined by gang activity, historical lines of hostility, and policing tactics. Bank and government policies like "redlining" have been used to create community boundaries related to race; examples like the Birwood Wall in Detroit still stand as monuments to that.

Every neighborhood has some type of boundaries. They may be different for different people and they may be flexible, changing as demographics change, but they exist. But if we want to reach the people around us with the gospel, we need to know the physical, emotional, and spiritual boundaries that group people together so we can minister to them effectively. The best way to find our community's boundaries is by doing informal research: walking an area, asking people, and observing.

DISCOVERING COMMUNITY BOUNDARIES

In the spring of 2016, we sent some freshmen college students out to find community boundaries in the Hunting Park section of Philadelphia. We thought this would be an easy task.

The students had been in that community on a regular basis for nine months and the boundaries seemed pretty clear to us. As we began the walk, we ran into a local church planter and thought, perfect! He had established his church only a few blocks from its mother church, believing that the neighborhoods were different, even that close together, and that he could reach a whole new people group. "Pastor Lin, could you please tell us your neighborhood's boundaries?" a student asked.

He hesitated. "Well, let me see. I think they go from somewhere over near Broad Street all the way to maybe Front Street, and from Roosevelt Boulevard maybe down past Hunting Park or maybe farther down." Not at all what we were looking for.

We tried again. "Pastor Lin, would your church neighbors feel free to travel on foot through all those areas?"

"Oh, no," he said. "They wouldn't usually go past 5th Street."

From this answer, it was clear that Pastor Lin knew his community boundaries well. He just hadn't understood our initial question, thinking it related more to how a city official might define a community on a map rather than how its residents would define the community's life.

In trying to define boundaries, a great question to ask community members is, "What are the boundaries you let your kids move freely in?" or "When you were a kid in this area, where were you allowed to wander?" My kids (Coz's) can go west from our house for about half a mile and north about the same, but no way can they go past the El station to the east or south past our block. If you came and walked the community of Frankford, where I live, the reason for this would be quickly evident. The drug dealing starts just to the east, and the south looks and feels very different from our own neighborhood.

Walking an area, talking to its people, taking note of what we see and hear, and sketching boundaries around our churches or target areas for planting a church is essential. It's also critical for us to be local churches that know the people and, more importantly, are known by the people if our goal is to make disciples in our areas.

Keep in mind, these boundaries may be different to different types of people. New residents to the neighborhood may not hold to historical boundaries, making it even more critical for us to understand who lives in our areas and how they function. Government decisions may influence boundaries as policies change. Housing developers and businesses will have an impact as well. But in the end, it is the people who live in our neighborhoods who should define the boundaries.

FINDING OUT WHAT GOD IS ALREADY DOING

Once we know the rough boundaries of our neighborhoods, next we must seek out what God is already up to in these areas. It might be arrogance that makes us believe that we are the first people to bring the gospel into our neighborhoods, but a theological position could also limit us from seeing what God has been doing. Most of us know historical stories of colonialism and imperialism as tactics used in conjunction with the church to conquer peoples. At times these took place with good intentions; but since it destroyed local cultures in the name of the church, it proved disastrous. God, through the Holy Spirit, has been at work since the beginning of time, and our role is to become part of the work He is already doing within the boundaries of our areas.

Recently, I (Coz) traveled to New Mexico with a group of students from Cairn University and we spent time in the Navajo Nation, meeting with local leaders and briefly exploring their culture. Many tragedies associated with government policies toward indigenous Americans have taken place, one of which was, alongside the church, creating boarding schools with the express goal of "killing the Indian to save the man."[1] The objective was to eliminate entirely all parts of the Navajo culture and replace it with white American culture. This was done by removing children from their families, creating physical and cultural boundaries between them, and placing children in these boarding schools. Harsh punishments were exacted on the children if they displayed Navajo cultural tendencies, including speaking their own language. Eventually, they were sent back to where they came from, where they were then disconnected and lost in their own communities. This damaged a culture beyond repair. Walking the streets of Gallup, New Mexico, one can see the ravages of a decimated culture: alcoholism, drug use, broken family structure, and lack of identity as a people group.

We can do similar damage to a local community when we come in and try to make people like us and fail to acknowledge the existing work of God through the local culture. If we want to find out what God is already doing in our communities, we should begin by asking ourselves: *What do I know about the other churches in the neighborhood where my church is located or where I intend to plant a church?*

If we don't know much, we should first go out and meet the pastors of the surrounding churches. Taking them to breakfast or to lunch, we can ask them to tell us their stories, share what they are passionate about, relate how they have seen God at work, tell us what encourages them and what challenges them. Even if we do not agree with them theologically or in practice, we can treat them as people created in the image of the King of Kings, called to do His work, as connected to God as we are, and experts in what they do. If we think highly of those already in a community, we will have taken one of the most important steps in effectively reaching a neighborhood—believing that the Holy Spirit is already at work.

After hearing someone's story, it is good to ask several questions:

- What are you doing to serve your community?

- Where do you live and where do your members live?

- What is the history of your church? Did it originate in your neighborhood or did you start elsewhere and move here because of the availability of the building?

- Is your church growing or declining in attendees?

Second, we can summarize what we've learned. Is this a community church or a commuting church? In what ways is it contributing to the harvest and serving the surrounding community? We shouldn't be surprised if we learn that neither the pastor nor most of the church's members live in the neighborhood. This is the overwhelming trend in churches around the country.

Finally, we can pray for the neighboring churches, as they will be one of our potential partners in the gospel harvest. We should keep them informed of what we are doing and ask them to keep us informed of their activities. We should never treat them like competitors for the handful of people who already attend church but as strategic allies in reaching the vast majority of people who won't be in anyone's church on Sundays.

Sometimes it might seem that there are already a lot of church buildings in our neighborhoods. But if we take the population of our neighborhoods and then subtract the number of people already going to churches (we will know this after meeting with all the local churches) or if we count the seats available in each church and see how small a percentage of our communities could fit in the churches if they all came on a Sunday, invariably we find that we don't have enough churches.

It's not just new church planters who need to be aware of what God is doing in a community. Established churches in an area also need to see what God is doing and wants to do through other believers. A few years back, a local church approached Common Grace, frustrated because their own denomination was launching a new plant in their community. It was within about five miles of their location and while the existing church had two services and showed continued growth, they were concerned that the new plant would have a negative effect on their attendance.

So we did a little research. We looked at boundaries, ran some advanced demographics, and looked at church makeup.

"How many people come to your church on a Sunday?" we asked the church leader.

"Three hundred to three fifty between two services."

"How many can you seat?"

"About three fifty each service."

"Did you know that sixty thousand people live in the

neighborhoods between your location and the location of the new plant? Even if you added a few more services, what percentage of this number could you accommodate?"

"Wow, we didn't know it was that many people."

"How many Chinese speakers are in your church?"

"Two or three, I think."

"Did you know that these neighborhoods have around ten thousand new Chinese immigrants in them? That's a lot of work for your three Chinese speakers."

"We didn't realize there were that many immigrants."

"What programs do you have for the disabled, since 10 percent of your community is identified as people having a disability?"

"That's something we haven't thought about too much."

"Okay, one final question. How many families did you care for last year who lost their homes in fires?"

"We did really well with that. We helped five or six families."

"That's great. But what about the other ninety-five families who lost their homes in fires last year? Maybe reaching your community is a bit beyond the resources of your local congregation and a new plant might help you in fulfilling your mission to reach your community with the gospel."

This church not only retracted their objections to the church plant but also began meeting the other twenty-eight local churches they found in the area and looking for ways to partner with them.

GOD IS ALREADY USING UNLIKELY VESSELS

If we can see that God is already at work, then next we can see that He is at work in and through vessels that are often unlikely and certainly unworthy. The Lord's choice of Paul as an apostle shocked the early church; and it took a special saint, Barnabas, to recognize the work of the Spirit in Paul's life and advocate that work to other believers. Despite Paul's history of seeking to destroy the early church (see Acts 7:57–8:3), he fulfilled the requirements God used to call people throughout history: the unlikely, broken, weak, and shameful. We see this in Jesus' choice of the other apostles (they were fishermen, tax collectors, and doubtful, angry men). We see it in prostitutes like Mary Magdalene. We see it in men like Moses, David, Gideon, and Jonah.

Like Barnabas, we are to seek out God's work in unlikely people, living in unlikely places, and bring this work to light so all God's people may rejoice. We need eyes that see not as man, but as God. We need feet of courage to go where many do not want to go. We need gentle spirits to encourage the most broken to share their stories of grace. The CUTS ministry is one example of what God has been doing through unlikely vessels.

Philadelphia is known for many things. It has played a major role in United States history. It is the home of Independence Hall and the Liberty Bell. Its sports teams and passionate fans are well-known. Christians around the world have heard of Tony Campolo and Shane Claiborne; and many know of Eastern University, Westminster Seminary, and Cairn University. Outside of Philly, though, not a lot of people have heard of CUTS. The Center for Urban Theological Studies holds classes inside a church building on the site of the old Connie Mack baseball stadium. It has no full-time faculty, no big library or cafeteria, yet it has been the central point for the academic development of pastors in Philadelphia for more than forty years. CUTS was born out of a small group of local pastors who came to realize that the church, particularly the black church, had a major lack of theological education (see Bill's story in chapter 3). When most of the major theological institutions moved out of the city, there was little opportunity for local bivocational pastors to take classes. The average age of a CUTS undergraduate student is forty-five; most have completed little or no college before enrolling, and some have no high school diploma. Some of the older students (those in their seventies and eighties!) still use mechanical typewriters, while younger ones walk in with iPads. CUTS won't deny anyone access to education based on financial position. Its leadership finds creative ways to cover costs. When we look across the city at effective, locally led ministries of all sizes, we almost always find threads back to CUTS. Whether a first-year student or a starting professor, CUTS has empowered local leaders by affirming their giftings, developing their skills, and offering them opportunities so often denied to those in poor urban communities.

Since before the beginning of time (see Eph. 1:4), God has been working salvation in people. Our role is to look for evidence in the places where we are called to serve and give praise and thanks when we find it (see 1:15–16).

When we fail to acknowledge that God is at work already through unlikely vessels in unlikely places, we cause many problems. First of all, failure in this area causes us to lack understanding of our communities, local leaders, and assets. Instead, we believe that only the outsider can bring hope to the poor and destitute. This paternalism leads to oppressing the local people and ignoring their spiritual gifts, since they are seen by the outsiders as spiritually inferior. This may take place with intent, although most outsiders are unaware of the harm they are causing, believing that because they are doing good works, things must be right.

Failure in this area also leads to a major disconnect between many churches and the youth of their communities. It is common to find young people relegated to their own part of the church with separate leadership and little integration into the larger body. In this way, youth are kept from positions of influence and power, limiting their ability to be effective agents of change. Statistics show that most people come to faith before the age of twenty-five, yet most leave the church between eighteen and thirty years of age.[2] Is it any wonder that the church has limited influence on the street, in schools, and in broken homes when those most open to changing culture are restricted in their access to resources and support? If we do not empower youth, then we cannot hand off power responsibly and we will continue to see churches close in the next generation.

Rev. Lou Centeno is an unlikely vessel being used by God. He is an invaluable leader in his north Philadelphia community, yet he receives little outside recognition. Many outsiders do their tour of duty in an inner city for a year or two, then back out. Others stay, usually gaining heroic status from those who send them, amazed that anyone could live in such dangerous places. Lou, a former gang member, grew up in his local community. The people there are *his* people, the ones he is commissioned to reach, no matter the cost. He is a first responder to crisis, empowering others around him, never seeking fame or credit. He exists on a meager salary—"too busy," as he puts it, to raise support. Lou is essential to the health of his community and, with more resources, would be able to do more work.

God is already at work—often in unlikely places, often through unlikely people—and we are called to look for that work. Upon finding it, we should give thanks to God, then share it with others in the body so they too may give thanks and be encouraged. We should then lift up the work, resource it as we can, and connect it to other parts of the body so that it may be lasting.

FINDING OUT HOW THE NEIGHBORHOOD SEES THE LOCAL CHURCH

After we see what God is already doing within the boundaries of our areas, often through unlikely vessels, we must ask our communities how they view the local church at large. We can talk to people on the street or knock on doors—not to do evangelism yet, but to ask people for their expertise as members of our neighborhoods. We can tell them that we are new in the neighborhood and seeking to grow in our understanding of our place, its people, and its needs.

We can ask people if they are regular churchgoers and, if they say yes, which church they attend. Is it located in the neighborhood or is it another area church? We can ask why they attend that particular church. If they don't attend a church, we can ask if they did previously and, if so, why they stopped. We should discuss their perception of the neighborhood. What are its needs? What are the key community resources available to them? Who are the significant community leaders?

We might want to talk with the leaders they identify to learn more. What can we conclude from these conversations? Which churches have real neighborhood connections? Is this a neighborhood of church attenders or an unchurched or de-churched neighborhood? We should not be surprised if we can't find a truly neighborhood-connected church. We also should not be surprised if we learn that the overwhelming majority of people don't attend any church or, if they do, that their church is located elsewhere in the region. Welcome to the church in America.

What has created this disconnect? Churches in cities and outside them today are largely commuter churches with little or no connection to their places. The community churches of the past are now difficult to find. As a result, community after community is left without a gospel witness. The local community rarely sees anything close to the face of Jesus. No wonder so few people attend church anymore—the Lord's people aren't doing His work in their world. The church in many neighborhoods is full of people who come in and take the local residents' parking places on Sunday mornings but are not a vibrant part of the local community's health and function.

Does anyone in our communities know who the church is and why we are there? If tomorrow we ceased to operate, would any of the locals miss us or care that we were gone? We agree with Dr. John Perkins, who argues that church leaders and members need to live where they worship and serve. If we don't, we'll never know the place nor will we connect to its people and institutions. The advance of the kingdom of Christ depends on the life and witness of every single believer. By making this our goal, a stated part of our church vision, we take a step closer to reaching every person in our communities.

DON'T BE IN A HURRY

Getting to know our communities' boundaries takes time, especially since they can be fluid or up for interpretation. It is easy to feel overwhelmed at the idea of meeting with other churches, let alone walking the streets, talking to neighbors, finding leaders, and engaging people. We may think the work of the gospel is so pressing that we don't have spare time to meet all these other church members who seem to have failed in the mission or obviously haven't done the job we now have to do. But we should stop and consider the Holy Spirit of God the creator and of Jesus incarnate. We are not alone in our work.

When we are planting churches, it is easy to feel that the clock is ticking. Church planters are often given three years of funding, maybe five. This is a ridiculous model that was established by many denominations and missions boards without thought to the local context many of us enter. These expectations are unfair, the pressure to "perform" is not helpful, and the failure rate of this model is, quite rightly, disturbing. It takes a year or two of living in a community before we can begin to understand that place and learn to communicate in it. Even when we are indigenous to our neighborhoods, we should take the time to look for things we may have missed or taken for granted.

We don't need to be in a rush. When we settle into our communities for the long term, we will be far more likely to reach new people with the gospel than if we spend our time church hopping. If we have been at church planting for a while, we may feel like Elijah: depressed, alone, wondering why God has called us to this place. But we can be encouraged. God has not forgotten us and He has set aside other servants, as He had with Elijah, whom He has called to Himself and who are already working in our areas. God will comfort us, strengthen us, and remind us of His power and glory to help us build relationships with other believers within our boundaries because in partnership with others, we will be far more effective than we can be on our own.

7

KNOWING OUR COMMUNITIES IN CONTEXT

We have discussed finding boundaries, getting to know what God is already doing within those boundaries, and learning how our neighborhoods regard the local church. Now we will look at knowing our communities further through what Common Grace likes to call "exegesis" of a neighborhood. This is important to understand if we are going to relate to the people in our neighborhoods and be able to reach them with the gospel.

Many people are familiar with the term "exegesis," one of those things seminaries like to teach. Formally defined, it is to explain or critically interpret a text and it generally means interpreting words based on the intent of the original author in context. This is in contrast to "eisegesis," which usually means reading a text without a sense of context or the intent of the original author.

When we study a community, it is important that we use exegetical techniques in context rather than eisegetical techniques from the outside without a sense of context. We must consider language, culture, tradition, history, and spirituality. Even though we may speak the same language as the group we are working with, if we are not indigenous to that culture, the way people use that language can be vastly different from our own familiar perspective.

Many church-planting organizations require significant Bible training, expecting their planters to be able to rightly interpret the Scriptures (which is essential), but they don't require their people to be able to interpret their neighborhoods in the same manner of excellence. In our personal observation, church planting has, of late, become a high-profile approach to reaching people. Denominations and agencies spend huge amounts of money to launch new plants, and many go into neighborhoods with almost no preparation at all to understand those areas. As such, their approaches tend toward attractional church models; and instead of church plants spurring on new gospel movements reaching unbelievers, they end up shifting existing believers from one location on a Sunday to another. When we take the time to understand our neighborhoods, we can become part of that neighborhood and effectively reach the people in that area in partnership with what God is already doing.

WALKING THE STREETS

After establishing boundaries, meeting with local churches to see what they are already doing, and finding out how the community views the local church, it is time to hit the streets again to gather more information. This is a great way to study a community in context rather than as an outsider. A number of techniques can be used to do this. Dr. Sue Baker at CUTS likes to refer to both "nonparticipant" and "participant" community walks.

In a nonparticipant walk, a person walks the community without interacting with any people. He or she takes along a friend or coworker, but the person is not trying to engage others at this time. One reason for this is that the individual is making observations based upon just what can be seen, not seeking interpretations from those in the area. A person may have to do this a few times and it is good to vary it—morning, afternoon, evening, different days of the week. The feel and demographic of a community can drastically change, depending on the time of day or day of the week.

Some years ago, Common Grace was approached by a second-generation Korean American church to do a demographic study on University City in Philadelphia, an area they considered to be their community. The church had numerous members who had spent most of their lives in the area. As we began the study, an African American church asked us to help them better understand their neighborhood. Surprise—it was also in University City and the two congregations had overlapping boundaries. As we spent time on the streets and examined demographic data, we found that the two churches could claim the same neighborhoods—but at different times. During the work week, many Korean Americans worked and studied in the community, walking the streets, eating at restaurants, building relationships. But from about three in the afternoon onward, African American kids returned home from school and adults came home from work; so in the evening the area was a residential African American community.

We brought the two churches together to think about what they could do together that they could not do alone. What resources did each congregation bring? What challenges did each face? It was exciting to see both groups acknowledge the presence of and need for the other.

Walking a community is the ideal way to begin to understand it. If we discover that an area is too large to walk, maybe the boundaries we have defined aren't accurate ones. Biking a community is also good, as it helps cover more area and can be a little less intimidating.

You might ask, why not just drive the area and get the job done faster since we aren't talking to anyone? Because being stuck inside a four-thousand-pound steel and glass bubble, we rarely pay close attention to our environment. We can't feel a community like we can when we're walking or biking. This is illustrated when a middle-aged white lady curses out her car window at a group of people biking along the street because she feels they are impeding her progress. The same lady wouldn't use that language if she met those people on the street walking. If they caught her at the traffic light, she would wind up her windows and keep her head focused straight ahead as if they no longer exist. Road rage, a sign of a major disconnect between people, is an example of how we miss what is happening around us when we drive.

Granted, in some neighborhoods we should be cautious about walking around. When working with students, Common Grace has specific guidelines for them to follow in certain areas until they develop the skills to walk there safely. As we transition from nonparticipant to participant walks, we should also transition which tools we use as we gather information. As an Australian, I (Coz) am usually in the ethnic minority most places I travel in Philadelphia. A good friend of mine once told me that if a person is white and walking through his community, he is one of the four Cs: a cop, a customer (buying illegal drugs), clergy, or crazy. A single white male walking through some sections of Philly's inner city stands out. A white guy walking his dog, however, appears more natural. Looking as though we belong can lessen the likelihood of encountering problems in a neighborhood wary of outsiders.

Taking children along can also be a great help for staying safe and blending in. I (Coz) almost always feel safer when I walk my children through a community than when I walk alone. With my kids, I am a dad doing what a dad is supposed to do; and even in the toughest communities, people generally respect that. From the outside, people perceive many poor communities to have little or no family values, but even when there is significant dysfunction in a community, people there usually place a high value on children's lives. When children are killed, the community mourns. When children are threatened, the community rises up quickly. Take as an example the prison rule of justice, where any pedophile incarcerated is treated violently by other inmates.

Another great way to safely walk any community is to walk with people who have lived there for a long period of time; this also lends itself to participant walks. We interact with people, ask questions, take notice of important elements, and see how our observations match up with those of the locals. If the people we walk with have been in the neighborhood a long time, you can point out things to them that they have become used to and they can see things from a different point of view than you do.

VISITING LOCAL ESTABLISHMENTS

Looking for appropriate opportunities to engage people is one of the most essential techniques for gathering information at a street level. Taking your kids to the playground and sitting on the bench as they play with other kids provides great opportunities to talk with other parents. Going to local stores, even if the products and prices aren't what we are used to, provides opportunities to rub shoulders with and engage local residents. As Dr. Eric Mason posted on his Facebook page, "If you don't know any places in your neighborhood to grab lunch, maybe you don't know your neighborhood."[1]

Patronizing local restaurants and stores can provide a wealth of information on your area, not only through those you meet in the stores but through the stores themselves. Common Grace gives the student groups who come to us this assignment: to find a local restaurant or supermarket owned by people from a demographic different from the current main one in a neighborhood and see if they can understand why it is there. Bustleton Avenue in Philadelphia has a series of Brazilian barbecue restaurants. Besides looking for an excuse to eat good, inexpensive Brazilian food, entering these restaurants can help people understand who may be moving into that area. The first time I (Coz) took my family to eat at one, I had never had an encounter with any Brazilians in my neighborhood. On entering the restaurant, a soccer game played on the television, a pile of newspapers stood beside the door, and the hostess asked me how many people were dining with us. All three of these were in Portuguese, Brazil's main language. None of the servers spoke English. As I looked around and listened to conversations, I quickly found that all the clientele was Brazilian.

The conclusion I drew, which was later confirmed, was that a significant population of Brazilians had recently moved into the area.

This can be contrasted, for instance, to an Indian restaurant that a group of students chose to visit in the Fishtown section of the city. Although there were some Indians in the area, they made up a small portion of the population and the restaurant owners intentionally marketed to the young, white population in that area. They were a mostly isolated Indian family rather than an indication of an Indian migration. Visiting local restaurants and markets is a fun way to engage and a great opportunity to explore a community through exegesis.

USING PUBLIC TRANSIT

Some church planters require their team members to use public transportation to get around. That can be an important element of understanding an area. Some communities have no public transit, though most have at least a bus that runs through them. In major metropolitan areas, buses, trains, elevated transit lines, subways, and trolleys can be the main mode of transport for a diverse group of people.

In his book *Code of the Street*, Elijah Anderson describes his trip on the number 23 bus, the longest bus route in the city of Philadelphia, as it traveled through racially diverse communities along Germantown Avenue. A person could have a similar experience by jumping on the El in Frankford in the morning, traveling into Center City, then out to Upper Darby just outside of the city. The experience would be even more informative on the number 7 in New York City, which has been said to be the most diverse public transit line in the world.

The experience actually begins just waiting at the bus stop. During a period of time in Nottingham, England, when I (Coz) worked in that area, I waited for a bus each morning and afternoon along with mostly the same people. The English were quite reserved and for a while I thought them a little rude, as I found it difficult to have conversation with them. After a week or so, though, people began to respond to my efforts and conversations took place. They had been watching me, seeing if I was just there for a few days or actually becoming part of their small community. Engaging people at bus and train stations isn't always easy; but if we really desire to get to know people in a neighborhood, it can be an important element of both gathering information and starting new relationships.

ENGAGING WITH PEOPLE

In all of these examples, we can perform informal interviews. We should prepare a list of basic questions before we go out and then find ways to ask those questions during a conversation or a series of conversations. They aren't scientific interviews but they can provide answers that many formal surveys cannot. There is an art to asking questions without letting people know that we are gathering information. It isn't meant to be deceptive or inauthentic. We are simply trying to figure out who lives in a neighborhood, how they function, what things are important to them, and how God is working in the area and in people's lives. Many neighborhoods will be suspicious of any outsiders coming in, especially if there is a racial or economic difference between the newcomers and the locals; so to be effective, we have to listen well, be patient, and stay conscious of how we are being perceived.

As white males in nonwhite communities, many times we are perceived for what we are not. Being mistaken for a police officer can make me feel a little safer and at other times quite the opposite—and it can even be quite funny. Once I (Coz) walked into the local place where I get my hair cut and asked if Maria was in. I didn't know the girl who was cutting another lady's hair that day, but I had known Maria for quite a few years.

"I'm sorry, there is no Maria here," was the response.

"Okay, when will she be back?"

"No, there's no Maria who works here."

"Yes, she cuts my hair."

"We have never heard of a Maria. Sorry, you are mistaken."

I took a short step back out the door and pointed to the large sign above it. It said "Maria's Hair Salon" in bright red lettering.

Still nothing. I turned and left.

Not long after, I got a call. "Were you looking for me?" asked Maria.

"Yes," I replied.

"They thought you were a cop. Come on over now."

I returned and the same girl who had "never heard of Maria" was still there. She just smiled and Maria laughed.

Not long after marrying my wife, Joyce, and moving onto her block in Kensington, I became frustrated as I tried to find out information on various incidents that had taken place in the area—a shooting, a robbery, an accident. My questions were mostly answered with, "No idea what happened." But in each case, Joyce would come home and proceed to tell me the entire story.

"How did you find that out?" I would ask her.

"I just asked people," she said. Joyce had been in the neighborhood a lot longer than I had and was engaged with most of the families through their children. She was a safe person, someone the people knew they could trust. I was just some strange Australian man. Later, I moved up to being "Miss Joyce's husband" and earned a little more trust.

Even though we will occasionally make mistakes, over time we can develop the art of asking informal questions in order to gather important information. In doing so, we can also begin to develop relationships.

There is a place, however, for formal surveys or questionnaires, especially early on. These are predetermined sets of questions by which we ask the same questions in the same manner to each person we encounter, generating a scientific set of data. We must remove as much of our own bias as possible when we form and ask the questions. We might begin with basic questions about age range, marital status, and employment and then move along to questions of lifestyle, beliefs, goals, and struggles. We want people to feel comfortable answering the questions, so it's important to explain who we are and why we are doing the survey. We also want people to know what we will do with the answers they give us.

One thing to avoid is leading someone to believe that we will act on their answers to solve some type of issue. For instance, we wouldn't say that our church wants to help change an issue in our community unless we already know that we have the resources to do so. It can be detrimental to relationships to set up expectations that we either won't or can't fulfill. We should employ this principle even in our local teams or congregations. Too often churches survey their congregations and lead members to believe that leadership will act on all their suggestions. When that doesn't happen, people can become disillusioned or feel as if leadership doesn't care about what they have to say. Still, it is helpful to practice surveys in our churches and think through how they may be perceived by locals.

Using a formal survey to get a foot in the door for a one-off encounter to share about our ministries, or even about God, is not a good idea. If we are doing a survey, it should be a genuine means of asking questions, not an icebreaker to tell people about Jesus. If we are truly committed to our neighborhoods, however, opportunities for deeper ministry will come and they will be more fruitful once relationships have developed.

GOING TO THE RIGHT PEOPLE

It is important to know how we will be perceived when doing any type of interview, formal or informal. I sent a group of students out to do informal interviews one day and they returned so excited. "Everyone we met was so friendly," they said. "They answered all our questions and some invited us to come back and ask them more questions tomorrow!"

"What was the general demographic of the people you talked to?" I asked.

"Mostly young men," they said. "We thought they wouldn't want to talk to us since we are from outside the area but they were all nice to us."

Did I mention that the group I sent out was made up entirely of college-age female students? And just a little naive! In general, we recommend sending mixed male and female groups, or encourage groups to focus on speaking to people of the same sex to avoid misunderstandings. In the story I just mentioned, the class was almost entirely female, leaving us few options.

But it reminded us of the need for a little more training of our students in this area.

These same principles are important in engaging children. It is not usually wise for a single man to approach young children in a community unless some type of relationship has been established with their parents. Making mistakes in these areas can be damaging and sometimes dangerous.

MEETING PEOPLE IN THEIR CONTEXT

All these methods are part of entering a neighborhood, going where people live out their lives, and engaging residents on their turf. This is in contrast to establishing an event or program on our own turf and inviting people into our world.

Decades ago, Young Life became a great student ministry. Its founder, Jim Rayburn, attended high school football games to get to know kids who would not turn up at Young Life's local churches. The ministry continues to model this idea of meeting people in their natural context. In Philadelphia, groups like the Barrio Youth Initiative require churches they work with to sign a covenant agreeing to work with youth in their context instead of requiring youth to conform to the church culture.

We should not have to stress this since Christ entered our world, met us in our brokenness, and moves us toward glory. So why do so many churches have a culture in which people don't feel welcome until they have it all together? Perhaps because we are too focused on events and programs in our own churches. These have their place, but neighborhoods are reached through authentic relationships that take place in resident's local context.

That's why Epiphany Fellowship in North Philadelphia built a playground on a vacant lot for the kids of its neighborhood rather than using their resources to build a fancy new children's wing at the church. It's why the member churches of Timoteo Football (we tell their story in chapter 15) won't mandate church attendance to play on their teams, but instead ask local church members to come out to the football field and support the players. It's why Maher Salhani, outreach director of Mariners Church in Mission Viejo, California, developed an intentional mission statement for their church. "When we meet people in their contexts," he told us, "our growing reputation in the community for support and care becomes a given. Public organizations knock on our door looking for us to help them in improving their community. This will prove, in the most tangible way, that the local church is the hope of the world."

He went on. "The biggest problems facing our society cannot and will not ever be adequately handled by politics or policy. God's people are swifter, more generous, more willing, and more joyful than the government could ever be. People outside the church will say of Mariners Church, 'They're what I thought Christians were supposed to be like,' because of our courageous work in the community."

Maher begins his strategy as we all should: sending team members out in our communities, surveying the landscape, finding out what is already being done, and deciding how the church can work as a partner to meet specific needs.

8

KNOWING OUR COMMUNITIES THROUGH STATISTICS

After spending an adequate amount of time on the street, in local restaurants, and in places where people hang out, it is time to gather in-depth statistical data on our areas. We cannot stress enough that this data needs to be specific to a neighborhood, not a circle you have drawn or a zip code (unless you are in an area where zip codes actually dictate community boundaries).

SOURCES FOR STATISTICS

There are many great sources of fairly accurate statistical data. The US Census is one, although for this you'll need your census block group numbers and it can take a little time to mine the information. In some communities, you can find data through university studies, school districts, local newspapers, and other agencies. Some groups offer community demographics for local churches. But again, unless we define neighborhood boundaries based on people movements that we have actually observed, the information is not useful for most places and, in many cases, can be misleading. It can be helpful to break a target neighborhood into subsections according to their residents, which you will likely discover through your time on the streets.

At Common Grace, we like to use information from a company called Esri (Environmental Systems Research Institute), particularly its geographic information system, ArcGIS. The software enables us to gather information on any part of the United States (and many other parts of the world) using our own polygon or predetermined boundaries (townships, counties, and yes, even zip codes). Many companies use this service to determine the market potential for a neighborhood and we have adapted it for the purposes of the local church. How we came to use this information is a story worth telling.

A developer began construction on a Target store in a section of Philadelphia generally known as Port Richmond. Although numerous stores existed nearby in a series of strip malls, Target just didn't seem to fit. Just south of the new store were many abandoned factories, the old river ward having fallen greatly since its heyday as a vibrant residential and industrial area where local residents also worked. Communities close by suffered from urban blight, failing schools, heavy drug activity, and violent crime. But not only did Target build its upscale store (for this area), the developer added a Starbucks—the only one for miles around. Perplexed and thinking that maybe Target was completely clueless, I (Coz) was even more surprised when Applebee's built not one but two restaurants in close proximity. Next came an Arby's fast food restaurant followed by the real stunner—a Cold Stone Creamery. Had everyone gone crazy?

It wasn't a Cold Stone community, it was a water ice community; it wasn't a Starbucks area, it was a Dunkin' Donuts area. We watched intently for these stores to fail.

But within two years, the community had changed. It had become a Starbucks crowd (well, a boutique coffee crowd, but Starbucks led the way). The area was gentrifying at a rapid rate, but not because of the stores. The stores had simply seen it coming well before we had. Our expertise took a bit of a beating, as did our egos. What had they known that we hadn't? Through a series of relationships, we began a conversation with a large-scale developer who, though not responsible for this series of stores, was building Targets and other big-box retailers around the country. An initial phone call, asking him how he knew where to build, led to him flying his demographics team out on their private company plane to meet with us.

He told us he was a fellow believer and said, "You know, you are the first Christians to ask me for my expertise in this area. Ministries always ask me to give money, but no one ever seems to want to know the things that made me money." We assured him we would be happy to receive any of his money, but what was more valuable to us was his knowledge. He and his team taught us how they gathered their demographic information, tracked trends, and predicted change. They explained why Walmart or McDonald's seldom fail—because they move to increase sales usually well ahead of the curve. They explained how they understand people movements—why people drive miles in one direction and won't travel a few blocks in another. They took what we understood about neighborhood boundaries and expanded it to a completely new level that we were then able to apply to the church.

We quickly saw that we could help churches know how their neighborhoods were changing, as well as predict what was coming next, by showing them how to find this kind of information. In cities where the average life span of a church is declining quickly, churches could finally get ahead of that trend. All this information is available to any church planter or church leader. Some of it—or at least the ease of use in gathering it—comes at a cost, but some is free and accessible if a person takes the time to pursue it.

Information such as housing prices can be gleaned from realtors, as this kind of data can rapidly change. Education attainment, travel times to work, age by race, and income by race can also be invaluable information. Data sources can include local school reports (in Philadelphia, local newspapers publish the "Report Card on the Schools" each year); crime reports (numerous sites publish this data, including local police forces, everyblock.com, and mylocalcrime.com); incarceration and release rates for jails and prisons (available at justiceatlas.org and by request from local county and state governments); and foster care and adoption rates (local county and state governments should have this information).

ANALYZING THE DATA

Once we have the information, we need to analyze it—look for trends, outliers, and movements. Reasons for the failure of an event for which we gave out a thousand flyers may become more evident when we see that the literacy rate is low or the flyer was in the wrong language for the literate. We may discover value systems when we see that people have four televisions per house but no college savings.

A recent study we conducted on a community we believed to be mostly gentrified instead revealed that, while the majority of households made more than $75,000 and 10 percent more than $150,000 annually, 20 percent of households made less than $15,000. That was a significant enough finding to notify churches in that area—including the growing ones that were attracting the higher-income earners—that the very poor were among them in higher numbers than they realized. They weren't rubbing shoulders with them at the cool coffee shops or creative pizza joints, and certainly their kids weren't attending the same kindergartens and nursery schools. These churches would need to either make some changes or encourage new partners to speak to this population, which included one of the most undesirable but significant groups to strategically reach—the elderly.

In community after community, we find significant populations of elderly people left behind when their native demographic moved on. If they are not already in a church, the likelihood of reaching them is very small. How often do we show up at the new church plant to see the elderly filling the pews? New church planters generally target a demographic similar to themselves, and we don't find a lot of elderly church planters coming into transitioning communities. Many people see the elderly as a burden or of little help in a mission instead of people deeply loved by Jesus and worthy of every moment it takes to share the gospel. The good news is for everyone and the elderly are vital to the mission of sharing it.

A former student at CUTS did his thesis project on a home care business for the elderly. Lance, an in-home hospice nurse, greatly impacted many of us at Common Grace as he told stories of holding the hands of the dying, people who were alone except for him—abandoned by family, with friends no longer around, and no church seeking them out if they weren't already part of a congregation. Lance now pastors a church in his spare time and sits on the board of a local health clinic, volunteering and reminding us not to forget this people group.

WHAT HAVE WE MISSED?

With this information in hand, it is time to go back to the streets. Walking, biking, taking public transit, both interacting with people we have already met and introducing ourselves to new people, we are now looking to see if the information we have gathered makes sense. Does the data support our observations? Hopefully it will; but if not, why? Could the data be inaccurate or could our observations be limited? Perhaps our boundaries are off by a few blocks.

Common Grace was studying a south Philadelphia community for an upcoming church plant. We knew the community was showing signs of gentrification and, when we were out on the street, what we saw supported that conclusion. But when we looked at the demographics, we saw a growth in one population where we had expected a decline. The new gentry group—older, wealthier African Americans returning to the city—was indeed expanding. It was the first time we observed growth in that area.

Oftentimes, as in the example above, the data alerts us to a people group we missed on our community walks. It could be the elderly who may be outside less frequently; it could be an immigrant group that works night shifts and sleeps during the day; it could be a non-English-speaking group that doesn't frequent the places we visited. We may have to go back and forth a number of times until we feel we have developed an accurate picture of a neighborhood and who lives and works in the area. As we do this, we are developing relationships with store and restaurant owners who are beginning to see us (and, hopefully, members of our church or team) on a regular basis. Local neighbors have been observing us, so we shouldn't be surprised if people start to approach us and engage us in conversation. All of this takes time but the investment is worth it.

SHARING OUR DATA WITH OTHERS

With a comprehensive picture of the community in hand, one of the first things leadership should do with this information is give it away. Approach other ministries in the area, or hold a gathering and present the data as a gift to them. This shouldn't be your first encounter with them; so it is an opportunity to thank them for helping you to begin, welcoming you into their communities, and being gracious in allowing you to interact with their church members. Even if you haven't felt welcomed by those churches, this is an opportunity for you to be loving toward them. When sharing the information you have gathered, you can also ask local ministers and neighbors how they perceive the data. Ask them: Do you think we missed anything? Do you have more to add? Is there anything that surprises, encourages, or challenges you?

If your experience is anything like ours, the data you find may leave you feeling a little discouraged. When we do statistical research, we often find more people, more diversity, more challenges, and fewer resources than we had hoped for. Perhaps we wanted to target a particular group and found that even if we reached all of those people, they would only equal 20 or 30 percent of the population. It is in those moments of potential discouragement that we should look around the space that we are sharing with other churches and see them as strategic allies in the work of the Kingdom. We are not alone. God did not call us to an isolated place where He has not already been at work. God has been and still is at work. We have an opportunity to build kingdom partnerships rather than operating in silos as competing tribes.

The complexity of our neighborhoods should inspire us to work together with others. This does not necessarily mean that we will do events together, exchange pulpit time, or hold combined services (though those things may happen). But, at the least, it should mean that we lead our congregations to pray for one another, share information and resources with each other, and work hard to never see each other as competition.

It is saddening, and at times angering, to see a new church plant arrive, begin spreading the message that it has come to save the community, spend almost no time meeting with existing ministries, and then watch people leave their churches for the new one without any conversations between the pastors. Instead of targeting the 80 to 90 percent of people who aren't in church, the new plant goes after the low-hanging fruit—the person who is already at church but may be looking for a different experience. It is a given that people will hop around churches, and that isn't always a negative thing; but when church leaders are not in conversation, it leads to a sense of competition that counters the concepts of kingdom.

In contrast, church leadership and planters should work together to provide a neighborhood with the sense of one God and one kingdom. Churches may worship in a diversity of ways and focus on a diversity of issues, but they are accountable to one another in fellowship. Working together may even lead to sharing resources with one another, setting aside funds (God's funds!) for the use of other churches. Most definitely, it leads to speaking highly of one another.

When we at Common Grace are asked, "Can you suggest a church to go to?" (which happens frequently), we love to list twenty or more churches where we think new people would feel welcome. We mention the churches we attend but we are not afraid to suggest others that may be a better fit. "You live in West Philly? You have to check out Sweet Union Baptist; they really know how to engage the community" or "You're looking for a more charismatic church? Bethel Deliverance is worth a Sunday morning visit. They have a comprehensive outlook on community and love to celebrate all Jesus is doing." If we truly believe that we serve the King of Kings, we must also believe that the entire fellowship of believers is His, not ours. If we want to see kingdom growth, not tribal transfer, we must act in a kingdom manner.

A CHALLENGE TO THE CHURCH

Northwood is an area near the geographic center of Philadelphia. In 2016, 13,723 people lived in this sixty-four-square-mile area. Some 29.4 percent were Caucasian; 47.9 were black or African American; 2.7 percent were Asian; and 29.2 percent were Hispanic. But no church in the community had this range of diversity in its membership.

As Common Grace planned a missional strategy for the area, we needed to find out which group each church in the area was seeking to reach. Who was missing from the churches? Where and how did these unreached people worship, if at all?

The median age in the community was thirty-one, which is relatively young for the city. Of great interest was the fact that 39.7 percent of the community was under the age of twenty-four. For most churches, this age group is a missing demographic. Also relevant, 95 percent of those attending church regularly in the United States came to faith before the age of twenty-five. How can the church grow without this generation? It is also interesting to note that some studies show that 75 percent of young people raised in the church stop attending between the ages of eighteen and twenty-five.

In the last sixteen years, homeownership in this area has dropped from 58.7 percent to 50.6 percent. The decrease shows that almost half the population now lives in rental housing. Because renters are much more transient than homeowners, this also meant that the stability of the community was decreasing.

A full 17.8 percent of households included a person sixty-five years of age or older. That is a significant percentage of the population often missed by the church. In addition, 36.9 of all households had one or more family members on disability. That figure could represent a range of disabilities but generally, this group is conspicuously absent from the church. Finally, only 12.4 percent of the households in this area have two parents living in the home along with children under eighteen years of age, and 21 percent of households have just one parent present with children under eighteen years of age.

Gathering statistical data is a powerful means of getting to know our communities and painting a picture of how we can reach out to the people around us. As the above information on Northwood suggests, the church needs to be thinking outside the traditional box when developing a missional strategy to reach every man, woman, and child.

9

FROM OUTSIDER TO INSIDER

While knowing our communities is vital to reaching people with the gospel of Christ, it is not enough. We need to move past knowledge of an area to identify with its people.

I (Coz) came to Philadelphia as an outsider, as did Bill. That can be a difficult challenge, especially when it requires a racial, cultural, or economic shift. But through our personal experience, Bill and I have discovered strategies for outsiders to effectively work in the communities where they relocate.

FROM AUSTRALIAN COUNTRY TO AMERICAN METROPOLIS

If you can find the city of Armidale, New South Wales, Australia on a map, you will realize that there aren't many places geographically farther from Philadelphia. The city is about ten thousand miles from Philly (sixteen thousand kilometers, for those not from America). Armidale has about twenty thousand people and is considered a city because it houses two cathedrals, the Catholic and the Anglican. It has a university and some good schools but in effect, it is a country town.

When I was eleven, my family moved to an area just outside of Armidale called Rocky River. It had a single street light, a public telephone booth, and a two-room schoolhouse that I attended along with the thirty-five other children who lived nearby. Most of the kids came from sheep farms.

Because my father was the principal, my family lived in the school residence. Armidale and Rocky River were surrounded by large farms and more than a million acres of state forest and national parks. They weren't anywhere near the outback; but compared to the northeast United States, it was the middle of nowhere.

In 1992, I moved into the Kensington section of Philly to work with Young Life Urban. I wasn't from a Christian home and had known Jesus for less than a year. I had no theological training, zero experience in youth ministry, and no financial support. I knew absolutely no one in Philadelphia except the Young Life city director and his two staff members. I was just dropped into one of the most challenging inner-city communities in the United States.

Early on, I planned to learn how Young Life was reaching young people with the gospel in Philadelphia and then take that learning back to my home country. That is what I had promised the youth leaders in Armidale. Twenty-five years later, I still carry some guilt for not honoring my promise. Perhaps they have done better without me anyway.

WHO IS OUR COMMUNITY?

I arrived in Kensington with my backpack, my passion, and my faith. I was taken into the home of Pete and Sue Carter, who not only housed and fed me but also taught me lessons that saved me from even more horrendous mistakes than I would eventually make. Pete and Sue are some of those unlikely people through whom God has done amazing work, but about whom few people outside Kensington ever hear.

My lessons came thick and fast as I encountered the gang culture of Philadelphia, brokenness of families, violence, drug abuse, and extreme poverty (by American standards). I learned from members of the community: youth, parents, pastors, families. Although I spoke the same language as the people I met, our cultures were a planet apart. In order to live in Philly, I needed friendships, mentors, supporters, and community. The local people provided all of those for me.

Who is our community, really? The vast majority of people who move from places of power into poorer communities maintain their primary relationships with people like them, whether those people remain on the outside or have also relocated into the new community. In simpler terms, people stick with people who are like them. So although a white "relocater" may now live in a majority Latino community, most likely his or her closest friends are still white. The argument is that we need people like ourselves in order to be sustained and places where we can get away from the poor communities we are in.

But this isn't the most effective way to do ministry or the most sustainable way to do life. If we can't draw sustenance from our local communities, then either we shouldn't be there or, more likely, we have a problem seeing who God is in people who are different from us. This could be a racial or an economic problem, but it is definitely a spiritual problem. When Jesus sent out the seventy-two, He expressly instructed them to draw their needs from the local communities they entered (see Luke 10:5–8).

Living life this way has to be intentional; it doesn't happen by accident. I had no Australian community to assimilate into when I first arrived in Philly. At that time, there wasn't an Australian pastor in the entire city. No Australian grocery stores, nowhere to buy a meat pie or a sausage roll. No footy (rugby league) on the tele (TV), no one inviting me to chuck a few snags on the barbie (barbecue), no cricket matches despite my searching (that has changed with significant Indian and Pakistani immigration). These were pre-Internet times and I couldn't look at the *Sydney Morning Herald* on my iPad nor could I afford to call home, so news took about two weeks to travel by airmail. I had to assimilate or get out.

INSTANT FAMILY

My initial work was on the eastern side of Kensington, an almost entirely poor white community where most of the youth I encountered were connected to some type of small gang activity. After about a year, I saw the need to work in conjunction with a stronger church-based ministry; so I moved across the railway line to begin working with Bethel Temple Community Bible Church, focused on reaching youth who otherwise wouldn't engage in church.

At Bethel, I met my wife, Joyce, who was running the children's ministry. Joyce came from central Pennsylvania. She was a graduate of Eastern University and had worked first in Bartram Village Projects in southwest Philly, then at Cornerstone Christian School, then in Santiago in the Dominican Republic. Finally, she made her way back to Philadelphia. Joyce was leading a movement of what would become many young women moving into the community, and she had built a strong reputation among local families as someone they could trust.

It took a while for me to convince Joyce to go out with me; I also had to win over her roommate, who was nine years old at the time. Joyce had taken in a young girl whose father was in prison and whose mother had gone away for eighteen months for help with her addictions. Later, the girl's brother joined Joyce when his father also went to prison. I remember so clearly the day this man (now one of my good friends) brought his son to Joyce. "Miss Joyce, you are the only person I trust. They are locking me up—please take my son." And with that, he left his four-year-old boy on the doorstep.

Joyce and I began dating; and in 1996, we were married—with two children. Those two (who are still close to us) spent the next year as our kids.

Not long after they left, a young teenager who was caught up in the drug trade moved in with us. After a few years, she left, got pregnant, went to prison, and left her then ten-month-old daughter in our care. Her stay has extended over eighteen years, as that little girl became our eldest daughter, Saiyeh. Not long after that, Melanie was born, then Emma, and finally Tony, completing our "regular" family at six.

But we have had no more than a few months without others joining us, from teenagers and college students to younger kids and single mothers with their children. It helps that I was in a community that saw family as a relationship rather than just a biological fact. That also had a way of taking in the stranger.

"PIMPING THE CITY"

I had strategic advantages, great mentors, patient teachers, and a community that was gracious enough to allow me to fail over and over again. Despite all this, I fell into the same traps most outsiders do and did some significant damage to my community along the way.

One summer, I was invited to speak at a suburban church in Michigan and, as all good missionaries do, I took along some local Philadelphians to share their testimonies. Those who joined me were working in the same area of ministry I was and we had known each other for quite a few years. They were articulate, talented, and used to outsiders. I shared that evening about our work in Philly, which at the time had received a lot of positive attention. I received a standing ovation, followed by many words of encouragement—and I am sure some money came in as well.

Afterward, one of my team members, Cindy Santos, approached me. Cindy is way more intelligent than I am (proven by her master's degree from Columbia in New York City) and, although she was just a teenager at the time, a simple conversation with her that day changed my world.

"Coz, you know why these people love you so much?"

"No," I humbly replied, although in my head was swimming, *Of course I do. I've given up everything—home, family, possessions—to move into a community that everyone else wants to get out of because I love Jesus that much.* I waited expectantly for Cindy to affirm how amazing I was.

"Coz, they love you so much because they think so little of me. You are their hero because you choose to live around people like me. How do you think that makes me feel? What do you think that's doing to my community?"

I was floored. Cindy was right. People were giving standing ovations and money because my family and I were willing to live in the inner city. It really was that simple.

How often do we hear about missions trips to the Hamptons (the posh east end of Long Island)? The vast majority are to people and places on a lower socioeconomic level than those who are going on the trips. Our friend Nes Espinosa, like many other local leaders, calls it "pimping the city." We justify it because in the end, people come to know Jesus, we spent money in positive ways, we handed out food, we ran a day camp. But we rarely consider the long-term consequences of what this does to a community.

Cindy set me on the path to understanding this dynamic. Other locals, like Nes, Ron Muse, Eric Desamour, and Hector Espinosa, stuck by me over the years to help me see things from their perspective. Hilda Mercado and Jazmine Diaz read anything I wrote and informed me of how their communities would read my stories—who the hero was from their point of view.

What became more troubling to me over time was seeing from demographic indicators that communities with a high rate of outside missionaries coming in were in fact declining, not improving.[1] The missionaries could tell all kinds of great stories, almost always with their ministries as heroes, but the areas where they served were getting worse. Why?

Well, it was quite simple. If we build ministries on the negatives of a community and raise money based on bad news, there is no incentive for us to change that story because doing so would limit how much money we could raise. If you send me money because I am sharing the gospel in a high-violence area, will you still send me money when we end the violence? If I tell you there are no other Bible-believing churches in my community so you should support ours, will I ever affirm the ones I do find or partner with them and risk losing your support?

I had never set about to hurt Cindy. Quite the contrary—I had sacrificed to help her. But I had done it the way *I* thought was best, rather than being informed by Cindy and her community the way I should have been.

EVERYONE NEEDS JESUS—NOT JUST THE POOR

One of the reasons this comes about is that we see missions as "us going to help them." We think they are worse off than we are because they don't know Jesus, at least not as well as we do, so we need to tell them about Him and help them become more like us. It is extremely difficult to see the strengths in a person whom we have already identified as needy, especially if that person is from a different racial group or lower economic status. This is a challenging thing to change.

In 2015, I took a group of college students on a trip to observe and listen to people ministering in Guatemala City. We began with a time of devotion led by our friend Joel Van Dyke, overlooking Central America's largest garbage dump, where thousands of people scavenge for their daily sustenance. Many students were moved to tears as they watched and most asked why we couldn't go down and do something for the people. Running a day camp for the children seemed like a good idea.

But no, I responded, we were there to observe. Later that day, we were in Cayala, a beautiful shopping complex for the wealthy of Guatemala overlooking the city. Students were relaxed as they window-shopped the designer stores and sipped their fancy coffees. I couldn't help but ask them, "Why no tears here?"

"Well, people here seem to have what they need," replied a student.

"Do they have Jesus?" I asked. "You seem to assume that those in the garbage dump are unhappy and need your help. Could they actually know Jesus and be content? And these wealthy people here, could they be depressed, anxious, lonely? Could they be filling their lives with material possessions to hide what only Jesus can fix?"

Now I do think we could help those in the garbage dump if they asked us, but perhaps what they would ask us to do is take their place for a day picking up garbage. Instead of running a day camp and becoming heroes to kids whose parents are out working to bring in food, we could allow the parents to have a day off with their children. The photos we'd bring back to the church wouldn't be of us playing with these poor, dirty little children who smiled and ran up to us. Maybe we could take photos and give them to the kids' parents so they could remember the day they didn't have to scavenge garbage. Maybe they would ask us for something completely different. We need to spend time with them to know what they would like us to do.

This assumption that the poor need Jesus is flawed. Everyone needs Jesus. Being poor does not necessarily reflect anything at all on a person's walk with Christ. When Common Grace helped to conduct a nationwide study on urban ministry, looking at key factors in leadership development, we asked a group of key

Philadelphia church leaders about their upbringings and how the factors that had helped form their leadership may have related to poverty. One interesting finding was that leaders who grew up in poverty all credited their upbringing for forming key components of their future leadership. They learned the need for collaboration when working with limited resources. They learned creativity by having to adapt what they had to what was needed to solve problems. They learned resilience through hardships. Despite all the negatives associated with poverty, it has been part of developing effective urban leaders.

GOOD INTENTIONS ARE NOT ENOUGH

Following Cindy's confrontation, I looked closely at the effects of outsiders on a community, asking questions of those who were born and raised there. I became more and more aware of the negatives coming from groups entering our community, whether through Common Grace or otherwise. Despite our efforts to do better training and preparation and have more local involvement, I found fundamentally that almost all short-term groups entering our community were causing more harm than good when they were evaluated from a native's perspective.

My frustration heightened around 2003, after our family moved from Kensington to Frankford. One day, I saw an all-white group of high school students in brightly colored matching T-shirts, knocking on doors as they walked down our street. When they got to our house, they invited our kids to come to their day camp in our local park, where the kids would hear about Jesus and have a great time. The group was from Ohio and had come, they said, because people needed to hear about Jesus in a place like this.

I found myself getting really angry. Thankfully, I didn't say anything and my wife reminded me it wasn't their fault. But I was trying to teach my kids to love their community, that it was a great place full of great people who loved God and served Him daily. And now here were these people who had come for a week. What did they think they had to offer my kids? What was their expertise in working in urban communities, in complex family structures? What did they know about our dynamics as a community? What did they know about our faith, our struggles, our lives? And after they played with my kids for a week and built relationships with them around Jesus, how often would they return to visit my children who had seemed so valuable to them?

When I was bringing groups to Kensington, I made the same mistakes those young people were making. I had repented from them, asked forgiveness for them, and tried to overcome them. Now I viewed those actions not as a missionary but as a father and a friend. We so often think that good intentions are enough when it comes to ministry, but coming into a community unprepared and inexperienced to run any type of program is like me trying to do surgery on someone. Doesn't matter how much I love the person or how much I love Jesus—I hope the individual would never let me near a scalpel.

It's different when an outsider enters into a submissive partnership with a local ministry, allows the local ministry to make all the key decisions, and helps that ministry's leader (although even this scenario can create some negative consequences).

This is why we started Common Grace. Each year, when students come to serve with us, I assign them a project to design a short-term missions trip for a visiting group from another country. Some students have a lot of fun with this and write parodies about the experience. Here's one example.

> The van pulls up on the beautiful street in the main-line suburb and the newly arrived team from Santiago exit the vehicle. They take photos of the houses, as they are so strange, and begin knocking on doors, asking if they could take the children to the playground for the day and play games with them. They also ask if they could help around the house, maybe mow the lawn or change some light bulbs. They try and take photos of the children they see and it all seems to be going well until the police arrive and take the team away for questioning at the station.

I mean, really. If a group of black and Latino youth from my community turned up in an affluent Philadelphia suburb and began knocking on doors to ask if children could come out and play, how long would it be before the police were called? Many others have written on these issues, such as Bob Lupton in *Toxic Charity* and Brian Fikkert in *When Helping Hurts*, but we echo their sentiments that good intentions are not enough for effective work in a community. The use of free labor to conduct a ministry ultimately costs the local community that people came to serve.

WE MUST BE INTENTIONAL

What are some things an outsider moving into a community for the long term can do to be integrated, build peer-level relationships, and become part of the local dynamic? Obviously, living in the neighborhood is important, so that its issues become our issues. When the garbage truck misses our block or strews trash along the street, it affects *us*. When police response times are measured by hours or even days, it affects *us*. When an abandoned home catches fire or street potholes are so deep that we worry about kids falling into one, it affects *us*. Christ entered our "neighborhood" to live among us; we should strive to do the same with those we seek to serve.

My family is a mixture of ethnicities. I am a first-generation immigrant, my wife is from central Pennsylvania, our eldest daughter is Puerto Rican (Austarican, she would say), and our other three kids see themselves as Australian-American hybrids. Our kids have lived their entire lives in a primarily Latino community in the inner city and they certainly wrestle with their identity in that regard.

Because I had no other family in Philadelphia, my wife and I built an extended family to help our children be well cared for, educated, and raised up in this complex environment. She and I have been intentional about bringing adults into our children's lives as well as about the ethnic, racial, and economic diversity of those we share life with. We chose a bilingual school for our children's K–8 education (they are all fluent in English and Spanish, with some Australian thrown in.) Our two younger daughters and our son were the only Caucasians in their grades; in fact, our middle daughter was the first Caucasian in her school. This hasn't always been easy; but research backs up the idea that being white in a nonwhite context, especially in poorer communities, is easier than the other way around.[2] We also chose a racially and economically diverse church, pastored by a Latino. Examples of weakness and brokenness are not hard to spot in our neighborhood, as drug dealing and violence are quite out in the open; hence we had to be intentional about showing them our community's strengths.

Our relationships were naturally with diverse people due to our work, so we invited them to help us as parents. We wanted to affirm our children's friends and their families and always make them feel welcome in our house. We didn't push our own kids to their racial identity but let them discover it for themselves. This led to some funny discussions, like when Emma—the palest person in her class—was voted class queen for the Puerto Rican Day parade.

"Dad, I like my class, but so many of them are liars," she proclaimed to me one day.

"Why do you say that, Emma?"

"Well, some of them were saying they are Latino and different from me, but that isn't true."

"And why do you think that?"

"Because we all look the same color."

"Oh really, Emma? And what color is that?"

Emma carefully examined her skin for a few moments. "A kind of pinkish, I guess."

That began her conversation on race.

Melanie, now in high school, attends a majority African American school and almost all her friends reflect that. She has had to deal with those friends' initial assumptions that because she is white, she must have come from the suburbs. She didn't understand it at first, especially because most of her black friends' families moved out of the city at some point but still define themselves as urban kids.

Our hope is to raise children who see every person as a creation in the image of God, who are gifted, and who have something to teach one another. But in American culture, this only happens through deliberately cultivated relationships. It doesn't just happen because we all love Jesus.

Although my kids don't always like the city and what life in it entails, they are a part of it. As a result, they do naturally things that have taken me years of deliberate action to produce. One day, when we were visiting a small farm out in Michigan and Mel had just gotten off a horse, I wondered what messages I might be communicating to our children since our holidays were usually around farmland. So I asked Mel, "How do you like it out here?"

"I love it," she told me.

"How does it compare to our neighborhood?"

"Well, it's much quieter, more peaceful, and there's lots to do. But I don't feel so safe here."

"What do you mean by that?"

"Well, Dad, if something out here was to happen to me, who would be around to help me?"

I thought of the week before when we had been at a Timeteo Football game in North Philly. On one side of the field had been a group of men from a halfway house, all of them felons, allowed to come and watch with their supervisors. The group of men on our side didn't look any different outwardly—all large black or Latino men as tough as the others. But for Mel, this second group was our family. Uncle Nes and Uncle Tony were there and Uncle Hector came by. Teo Luis wasn't far away and Titi Hilda would be over in a minute if there was trouble. My children saw these men not as people to be feared but as protectors and providers. My kids can easily recognize trouble and who will cause it, but it isn't based on race or economics.

All this is a result of being intentional in how we do life. Making these decisions isn't easy and not everyone is called to live in a challenging neighborhood. Finding quality education or a quiet street with solid policing is, for many people, reason enough to move out of the city. But for those who do relocate to an urban neighborhood, what message do we send the local residents when we aren't willing to share our lives with them and allow them to share theirs with us? When they see us leave for Christmas and Easter? When we are always open to listening to their problems but never tell them our own sin struggles or failures? When we don't look to them in our times of crisis but run back to where we came from or to people like us?

Our community members need the opportunity to speak into our lives, confront our sins, celebrate our strengths, help us parent, protect our families, and give and receive.

THE BLESSING OF POVERTY

Poor communities have been gifted with an abundance of grace. In more than two decades of life here in Philly, where I have tried to make people "better," those same people have accepted and loved me for who I am. I rarely feel judged in my community. My failings as a parent and husband are accepted (though people offer encouragement and give advice when asked). I don't feel pressure to send my kids to a certain kind of college or have them in the best sports or music programs.

My community has embodied Matthew 25:31–40, where Jesus speaks about the people coming into eternity with

Him—those who gave the thirsty a drink, housed the homeless, and visited the sick and imprisoned. I hold that in poor communities, no matter the level of dysfunction—violence, drug abuse, or brokenness—we find people who answer the door when we knock. Who share what little they have. Who offer a cool drink, some food, and even a place to stay. They visit their friends and family in prison often. They live Matthew 25.

How do many of the good church families in the supposed well off communities respond to the same knock on the door? Would they give you a meal? A place to stay? A visit if you were locked up? There are benefits in making our homes and lives in the neighborhoods where we seek to minister. We must allow these communities to care for us and become our friends and extended family. If we usually call these communities poor or broken or dangerous, let us become open to the amazing things God is doing and will continue to do in unlikely places through unlikely people created in the image of the King of Kings.

PART 3

THE PROCESS—WORKING TOGETHER TO REACH OUR COMMUNITIES

10

EVERY PERSON GIFTED AND NEEDED

In order to truly live the gospel in our communities, we must be spiritually mature believers. Growth to maturity is the responsibility of the whole church, and the gifts of every single member are essential to that growth. We will not grow to maturity without ministry to and from each other. We need each and every person in the body of Christ if we are going to partake of this thing we call growth to maturity in Jesus.

The body of Christ should be a place where every member welcomes others with the gospel, every member is maturing in Christ, and every member is using his or her gifts for ministry. We should work to be a body in which all of us are maturing in the Lord, sharing our faith with the people in our lives, and using our gifts for ministry. If any one of us decides to sit on the sidelines, something will be missing from the puzzle. Nobody is extraneous to God's redemptive purpose.

The apostle Paul tells us in First Corinthians 12, "Just as a body, though one, has many parts, but all its many parts form one body, so it is with Christ. . . . You are the body of Christ, and each one of you is a part of it" (1 Cor. 12:12–27). One body, many parts together. God designed the church in this way for the business of growing us to maturity in Jesus.

CHRIST GIVES GIFTS TO HIS CHURCH

Paul makes clear to us in First Corinthians 12:12–27 that there is one body, not many bodies. To help us understand, he points us to the unity of the Godhead—Father, Son, and Spirit (see 12:4–6). He talks about how the ministry of the church is not a human endeavor, first of all. When we worship on Sundays, we see ushers serving, volunteers in the nursery caring for the children, people driving others to the church. But the ministry of the church is not yours or mine—it is God's.

Paul tells us that what is going on in our ministries is headed by God and it's God who leads the way in working in the body. It is God's Spirit who called each of us to Himself and placed us in the body. The messenger didn't give us the gospel—God's Spirit tuned our hearts to hear the message and united us to Jesus. God led us to the particular places where we are rooted in the body. God placed us there for our growth in the Lord. For that reason, He gives gifts to the church. Ephesians 4:11–16 tells us that Christ is the head and as such, one of His jobs is to give His people gifts for ministry. Those gifts go not to one or two people, but to every single believer in the Lord.

Paul tells us in First Corinthians 12:6 that "there are different kinds of working, but in all of them and in everyone it is the same God at work." God doesn't enlist different spirits to work in different places. His Holy Spirit works in all places where there are believers: "All these are the work of one and the same Spirit" (1 Cor. 12:11). Our oneness as believers comes to us because of our union with Jesus. When we think of each other in our local congregations, we see that we are many different people. We look different from each other, we dress differently, we think differently, we act differently. But one common thing unites us all and that is a relationship with Jesus Christ. That provides the church with an essential unity in the body. What God is doing in our own churches is really no different from what He is doing in any other part of the body of Christ. In every part of His body in this world, wherever it is, God is working the same grace and maturity in the lives of His people.

Our failure to understand this is one of the greatest hindrances to the growth of the body. God Himself is leading and uniting the church.

THE CHURCH IS THE BODY OF CHRIST IN THE WORLD TODAY

When we think about the body of Christ, we first think about Jesus' body, how He lived His life on the earth, and His sacrifice to die on the cross. This should help us think about our life together as His body now. We can learn a lot about being Christ's body if we study Jesus' life, because we are partaking right now in our corporate life of that same life that He lived. He isn't doing anything different today from what He did when He walked on the face of the earth.

Take, for example, the books of Luke and Acts, written by Luke, who was a helper of the apostle Paul. In Acts 1:1, Luke tells us, "In my former book, Theophilus, I wrote about all that Jesus began to do and to teach." The implication here in Acts is that Luke is going to tell us about what Jesus continues to do and teach in His church.

In Acts 1:9, we read that Jesus ascended to heaven, and some might say that Jesus' work on earth is done. But that is wrong! Jesus' work in His physical body was done, but He continues to do the same work in us now as He did in His church then. He gives us the Holy Spirit in full measure to accomplish that work in our lives. What Jesus did, we now carry on. It is no different in kind, although it is greater in extent today than it was when He was here on the earth (see John 14:12).

Too many of us think that our growth to maturity would be a done deal if only Jesus were living here among us. But the truth is, He is. He is living among us in a better way than He did when He was bodily here on the earth. He comes now and doesn't sit next to us or in front of us or behind us, but He resides in us. That way, He is able to be with each and every one of us twenty-four hours a day, seven days a week. There is no time when Jesus leaves His post of ministry in the body. I can't think of anything more wonderful than that. He is continuing His same work.

So when we think about the body of Christ, we can have a larger picture than that of Jesus walking the roads of Galilee and Jerusalem. Jesus is now walking wherever there are believers. As we walk the streets of our neighborhoods, Jesus is there walking with His people and accomplishing the same things He did yesterday. We can think of ourselves as the embodiment of Jesus in the world today.

If we think about that in terms of ourselves alone, without being connected to others, we are in trouble. But when we are connected to each other in Jesus, one plus one is more than two.

The body, in its fullness, is the very demonstration of the life and the power of Jesus in the world. This is why Jesus, in that great prayer of John 17:21–23, essentially prayed, "Father, make My people one, even as You and I are one." Why? "So the world will know that You sent Me."

There is nothing more powerful in its demonstration of the divinity of Christ than the unity of believers in the church. We are a motley crew of people who come from many different stations of life, from different points of brokenness. But Jesus met us and brought us into His body. As people see our lives together, they see the demonstration of the power of God in us. This should lead them to say, "This is not a human endeavor. It must be of God."

We are Christ's body in the world today; and it is through us that Christ is accomplishing His purposes in the world—reaching the lost, vindicating His name, building up and nurturing the saints, making us servants to the world in the name of Christ.

THE CHURCH IS SINFULLY DIVIDED IN THE WORLD TODAY

This truth applies not just to individual believers within a local church but to churches within a community and beyond. But oh, how we have divided up the church.

Common Grace sees thousands of churches in Philadelphia. A lot of Christians laugh at some of those churches just as much as the world does. We go around in our vain superiority thinking that we alone have a corner on the "Jesus thing." But wherever His name is confessed, Jesus is at work. He may be doing things a little differently in one place than He is in another.

Sometimes His people may be weak. Sometimes they may be struggling. But every church is still the work of Jesus.

This is a lesson that has taken me (Bill) a long time to learn because I was taught to look at the church and see not one body of Christ but Presbyterians, Baptists, Episcopalians, and Pentecostals. To see black and white in the church. To see Norwegians, Dutch, Spanish, Korean, and Chinese. I was not taught to see Jesus in His great diverse work of reaching people everywhere. But as we drive around our cities and see all those little storefront churches and all those large megachurches, we are to remember that our brothers and sisters in the Lord are together with us in the army of God in reaching this world for Jesus.

We have divided up the church in terrible ways. Too often our political affiliations or denominational differences are more important to us than our essential unity in Christ. When we look at the church around us, we are to see that we are partners together in the body of Christ. We are together salt and light. If the light in Philadelphia were limited to the light of a single congregation, how dim it would be! But the light in Philadelphia is made up of all these parts of the body, and what an army it is! What a bright light it is! It is daylight in Philadelphia all the time when we understand it from that perspective.

That doesn't minimize our differences. But the differences we have are minor when compared to the work of Christ in the world. And all of them are surmountable as we come together in humility before the Lord with an open Bible in our hands and say, "Teach me, Lord. I want to learn from You." One body, and only one, in the world. We are to see and understand our essential unity first with Christ and then with one another.

This body has many parts to it. Some of these are man-made—Presbyterians, Episcopalians, Baptists, and Pentecostals. There are both negatives and positives when it comes to understanding the place of denominations in our world. Denominations are helpful to the mission of the church when they enable local churches to work together for the mission of God. Denominations are not helpful when they keep us from partnering with other parts of the body of Christ. Too often, we only work with churches in our denomination. This can just as easily keep familiar parts of the body from working in connection with other, more diverse parts of the body.

The urban church today is finding new ways of partnering in missional outreach for the blessing of our common community. Churches are working together to address educational issues, the problem of alcohol and drug addiction, housing for the homeless, or ministry to street youth. Churches today are learning that they can do more together than they can when they act alone in a vacuum.

But some of the various parts in the church are God-created. When Paul tells us that there is one body with many parts, he is talking about gifts—ministries that God gives to each member of the body of Christ. God gives us a diversity of parts in the body, because a diversity of gifts is needed in the ministry of the church in order for growth to happen. Paul wants us to grasp this as we think about the church, so he gives us two lists of these gifts in First Corinthians 12. They are not intended to be exhaustive, but a template against which we can begin to think about all the different gifts that God has given to the body of Christ for our growth.

EVERY GIFT MATTERS

As we saw earlier, the Word of God teaches us that each and every member of the church is a minister. It's not just the pastor who does the work of ministry; we all are ministers in the body and each of us has been given gifts for ministry. Each of our gifts matters to the rest of the body's growth.

In First Corinthians 12:22, we see that some gifts are "weaker" gifts. Some just do not have a lot of strength and do not seem to amount to a whole lot. When we see these, our prejudices come out and we want to rank some gifts as more important than others. But Paul tells us that no gift is more important. We say that sweeping the floor on Saturday night, well, that is a weaker gift. But go six or seven weeks without sweeping the floor and we might reconsider whether we think sweeping is a weak gift. We may not see it at work, but it is there and it is essential to our life.

In verse 23, Paul refers to "honorable" parts, gifts we naturally acknowledge and celebrate. I (Bill) am often asked to preach at pastors' anniversaries—do churches ever honor their pastors! But I've never been to a service honoring ushers or secretaries or prayer warriors. By nature, we honor the visible parts, the ones who stand up and preach. As a preacher, I am taken care of every week. Sometimes I receive a nice paycheck. Other times I am told, "That sure was a good sermon." I walk out, my head is swollen, and I think to myself, *Boy, they really understand that I am one of those honorable parts!*

But there are other parts of the body that we never honor. One of the beautiful things about this, though, is that since Jesus is the One who gives the gifts, in the ultimate sense, it is Jesus who gives the honor. Those gifts that we forget all the time, God tells us in this passage that He takes care of them. In line at the awards ceremony in heaven will be all those saints who never got a word of commendation in the church. Jesus will lead that procession.

We must learn how to make a distinction between presentable and unpresentable gifts. We look at the person who doesn't dress elegantly. We decide that when a presentation needs to be made, we won't choose the person wearing a shirt from the 70s to do it. We care about our appearance, but God doesn't. He is looking at the spirituality, the inner parts, and the ministry of connectedness in the body. Gifts are His presentation of Himself to the world, and He often uses the little folks of the world to shine on the big folks and show them what real love is all about. He uses the person who, when put in front of a group of people, can only stutter. Yet the message that person conveys with his or her life and words expresses the deepest understanding of God. Is it our eloquence or our content that counts?

HOW ARE WE LINKED IN THE BODY OF CHRIST?

We are members together in one body, and each one of us is essential to the life and the growth of that body. You are essential to my growth and I am essential to yours. Paul tells us in this First Corinthians 12 passage that there are two things we may never say to each other when we are in Christ: "You don't need me" and "I don't need you."

In the paradigm below, which type of linkage best describes you?

UNATTACHED	I don't need you	You don't need me
DEPENDENT	I need you	You don't need me
INDEPENDENT	I don't need you	You need me
INTERDEPENDENT	I need you	You need me

Unattached. This first category describes people who think they can be unattached in their relationship with the body. They only attend church occasionally and seem to say, "I don't need you, and you don't need me. I will come and get what I want when I want, but don't count on me for anything. You have no contribution to make to me in Christ and I have no contribution to make to you. I have a relationship with the Lord and that's all that counts." But there is no such thing in the family of God as an unattached family member, even though some of us function that way.

Dependent. Then there are the dependent folk. All of us were at this point at one time or another. New believers start in a position of dependency. We all sing as we come to Christ, "Just as I am without one plea but that Thy blood was shed for me." We come with a deep sense of our sinfulness and emptiness, of how we need Jesus and have to catch up in our growth. We need other Christians, but we think we will never make a contribution to the body of Christ. In this category we believe, "I need you, but you don't need me. What do I have to offer?" Some people stay here a long time. Some people never move to the next step.

Independent. This next step is where I find myself most of the time and this is still a problem for me. These are the Christians who say, "I don't need you, but you sure need me." They walk alone in the Lord. They don't need little checkups. They are always there on Sunday so people can never find them delinquent. The body can count on them, but they sit there with this sense of "You need me, but I really don't need you. I could get on just as well without you. I don't get bent out of shape about what I don't get taught because I can go and figure it out for myself."

I grew up in a home that taught me to be independent and part of that is having a strong ego that says, "Boy, the world is surely blessed because of me, but I sure don't need anyone else. In fact, if I start counting on people, they'll drag me down! I'm not going to get too close to anyone because if I do, I'll get in their mess and that will divert me from my purposes. Who needs all of that grief?"

I am thankful for a couple of saints in the body who came to me recently and said, "You are awfully detached around here. When are you going to start attaching?"

I said to them, "I don't need it."

Then they said, "But we need you."

As I reflected on that, I realized that the position I was taking was just as unacceptable as that of the unattached person because I was negating and badmouthing Christ's work in the body just as much as the person who only occasionally shows up at church.

Interdependent. The Lord doesn't want us to be unattached or dependent or independent. Instead, He calls us to interdependency. That person says, "I need you and you need me. We have ministry to do together in this family." In this picture of interdependence, we share each other's strengths to meet each other's needs. When we do this, we all get stronger. We don't pool our dependency; we pool the richness of God's grace in our lives for the benefit of all. Paul talks about this in First Corinthians 12 when he says that God gives gifts to the church for the common good.

GROWING IN INTERDEPENDENCE

The Lord asks us to consider our relationship with the body of Christ. Are we growing as interdependent people with the other members of the body?

In a discussion about these things, a good friend of mine told me that she fits into all the categories at different times of the week, month, or year. Sometimes she chooses to detach from the body. Other times she functions dependently, knowing she needs others but having lost the sense that they also need her. At other times she becomes independent and feels that she doesn't need others. She fluctuates between the three and needs help moving to a consistent walk in the biblical place of interdependence within the body. This is the challenge to you and me.

A lot of us make the false assumption, "Well, I'm growing and that's all that counts." But Ephesians 4:13 tells us that we are to keep on ministering in the body until we all come to the fullness of Jesus. Some of us may be blessed to come to complete maturity in Christ on this side of glory, but that does not give us the right to sit down on the sidelines. To those who are given much, much is expected. They should contribute to the growth of the body because what they have was not given to them for their own endowment but for the enrichment of the ministry of the body of Christ. It is in that ministry that all of us grow together.

Saints of God, catch the vision that growing to maturity in Jesus is not impossible. Jesus leads the way in this ministry and He has given to each and every one of us gifts to grow to the fullness of Christ. We must consider before the Lord what our calling is in this ministry. Nobody is exempt. As we discern the work of the Lord in our lives together, the body of Christ will become stronger and richer and more blessed and more strategic in its ministry to the people around us for the praise of God's glorious grace.

May we learn this lesson in the very depths of our being!

11

BRINGING GOD'S PEOPLE TO MATURITY FOR SERVICE

Every believer, as we have seen, is called to be the hands and feet of Christ in our communities. This is not the job of just the pastor or church elders. God wants every one of us to be disciples who follow Him in whole-souled obedience in every area of our lives. God has designed the church to be a place where sin-broken people are rebuilt from death to life and nourished and discipled over the course of their lifetimes. When the church functions this way, each believer matures into the likeness of Christ and is then able to minister to others.

How then do believers attain this maturity? This is where the role of church leadership comes in. Our job is to equip believers through the Word of God so that each one will be mature in Him and able to live the gospel in his or her daily community interactions.

THE FIVE EQUIPPING GIFTS

Ephesians 4:1–16 explains how God has organized the church to reach its goal of attaining maturity in Christ. The church, until very recently, has misunderstood this passage to a large degree. This misunderstanding has led the church to have an unhealthy dependence on its ministers.

When believers are asked, "Who are the ministers in your church?" many traditionally name one person: the pastor. Believers have looked to the pastor to do the work of ministry. Frequently this has meant that all the rest of the church had to do was "pay and pray." This has led to an unhealthy imbalance in the church, and it is one of the reasons that the majority of churches in the United States are quite small. They are dependent on the labor of one, maybe two people.

God tells us that ordained ministers do indeed have a vital role to play in the church. But we need to be clear about one thing: Every member in the body is a minister in the church. If the body is to function in a healthy way, each and every one of us must take our part in the ministry (see 4:16).

The misunderstanding of this passage occurred quite simply. It has to do with the placement of a single comma, which makes all the difference in the world. For Ephesians 4:11–12, most translations of the New Testament before the 1960s followed the translation of the King James Bible. He gave some, apostles; and some, prophets; and some, evangelists; and some, pastors and teachers; for the perfecting of the saints, for the work of the ministry, for the edifying of the body of Christ.

Because of the way the commas are placed, the function of the apostles, prophets, evangelists, pastors, and teachers was said to be threefold: 1) perfecting the saints, 2) doing the work of the ministry, and 3) edifying the body of Christ. It was considered the job of those who had these special gifts to do all three functions.

After 1960, all translations followed the same basic translation we now find in the New International Version. In these translations, the first comma in verse 12 (after the word "people") is omitted. Christ himself gave the apostles, the prophets, the evangelists, the pastors and teachers, to equip his people for works of service, so that the body of Christ may be built up.

Now the passage essentially reads, "Apostles, prophets, evangelists, pastors, and teachers are to prepare God's people for works of ministry." See the difference? The leaders are not to do the work of ministry all by themselves but rather prepare the whole body for its work of ministry so it will be built up until we all reach maturity. The work of ministry is not just the work of those who have the special gifts but rather of everyone in the body. What a difference one comma makes!

There are a few supporting reasons for saying that this is the preferred translation. In Ephesians 4:7 we read, "To each one of us grace has been given as Christ apportioned it." This gift of grace does not go only to those who have the special gifts but to the whole body. You'll notice also in verse 16 that we are told, "From him [Christ] the whole body, joined and held together by every supporting ligament, grows and builds itself up in love, as each part does its work." The body of Christ will grow in the proper way only as each and every one of us takes up our work of ministry.

THE JOB OF LEADERSHIP—EQUIPPING GOD'S PEOPLE

The gifts of apostles, prophets, evangelists, pastors, and teachers have a special function to prepare God's people for the work of ministry. These words—"preparing" or "equipping" or, in the King James Version, "perfecting"—are important for us to understand. They literally mean "to bring to perfection" or, in today's vernacular, "to tune up" the people of God into the fullness of Christ.

Let me give you an example. Your car isn't running properly, so you take it to your mechanic. He or she tells you that the car needs a tune-up, which may mean that your engine's gasoline system is not cooperating with the electrical system. The engine is designed so that the gas gets into the cylinder at the same time the spark from the ignition wire gets there. If that gas gets there late or early, you have problems. You need to bring all the systems in the engine into sync with one another if the engine is going to function properly. It's the mechanic's job to bring the engine's systems in tune with one another.

In like manner, the jobs of apostles, prophets, evangelists, pastors, and teachers are to tune up the body of Christ so we are brought into conformity with Jesus. They are generally, though not exclusively, found among the elders in the church. These special gifts are primarily ministries. In other words, those with these gifts are supposed to deliver the Word of God to the body of Christ, each of them in a distinct, unique way. It is only as we function on the "Jesus operating system" that we will grow to spiritual maturity. If we are out of sync with that, the body will not grow.

APOSTLES AND PROPHETS

The apostles and prophets are those who first give us the word of the gospel in proclamation and then in the inscripturated—or written—Word, which is the Bible. Paul tells us in Ephesians 2:20 that the church is "built on the foundation of the apostles and prophets, with Christ Jesus himself as the chief cornerstone."

Paul was an apostle in that he was a direct eyewitness to the resurrection of Jesus Christ and commissioned by Christ to preach the gospel to the Gentiles (see Gal. 1:11–24). The early church questioned the apostleship of Paul because at the time when Jesus rose from the dead and before He ascended, Paul was Saul, the persecutor of the church. When he began to be known as the apostle Paul, people said he couldn't be an apostle because he could not have been an eyewitness to the resurrected Christ. Paul acknowledged that he was not a witness of the resurrected Christ in that period and had indeed persecuted the church. But he asserted that he was an eyewitness to the resurrected Christ in the event that took place on the Damascus Road when he was going to imprison Christians who were fleeing Jerusalem (see Acts 9:1–30; 22:1–21; 26:12–23; Gal. 1:11–17). There he met the resurrected Christ. As an apostle, the word that he preached and wrote carried God's authority with it (see 1 Cor. 1:4–2:5).

The apostles began the work of establishing the church by giving us the word of the gospel; they told us with certainty that Christ had risen from the dead and become the firstfruits of all those who believed. But their work was not finished as apostles until they had written that word down in a form that could become the living Word of God to His church throughout the ages. The word of the apostles, as the written Word of God, is the foundation of the church (see Eph. 2:19–22).

The reason Christ is the chief cornerstone is that all Scripture, made up of the Old and New Testaments, points to Jesus. It is Jesus who holds it all together. The Old Testament points ahead to His coming. The New Testament announces that He has come and fulfilled the Word of the Lord, and points ahead to that great and glorious day when He will come again. The prophets of the Old Testament served the same function before the coming of Christ. Their preached word called the people of Israel to repentance and faith, and pointed ahead to the time when God's Messiah would come to save His people from their sin. Likewise, their word was inscripturated in the books of the Old Testament, and this Word served as the foundation of the faith life led by the Old Testament people of God. This was so because it bore the very authority of God Himself (see 2 Pet. 1:16–21).

EVANGELISTS

The third equipping gift is that of the evangelist. The evangelist has the unique capacity to preach the gospel wherever the Lord leads. All of us, if we are believers in Jesus, are to be His witnesses, but certain believers have a special gift of evangelism that we must understand.

Most of us would never have heard the word of the gospel had there not been evangelists. The gospel began with the Jewish people who, in and of themselves, had no capacity, desire, or inkling to preach to the Gentiles. The Gentiles were unclean. The Lord had to come to the church and commission a body of people to carry the gospel across those barriers and say to the Gentiles,

"To the Jew first, but also to you who are Gentiles" (see Rom. 1:16; 2:9–10). Over the centuries, evangelists have heard and responded to the call of God to take the gospel where it has never been before. It requires learning to speak the languages of other people so they can hear the gospel in their own tongues. It requires making cultural adaptations so that when evangelists go from one people to another, they don't impose their own habits or traditions.

The early church fought long and hard over whether the Gentile believers needed to be circumcised. This issue controlled the agenda of the church for a period (see Acts 15:1–35; Gal. 2–5), and it divided many Christians because some insisted that Gentiles must become Jews in order to be part of the believing community. Paul, on the other hand, fought long and hard as an evangelist to say, "No, the gospel does not require one to become a Jew in order to come to Jesus. You can come straight to Jesus." Jesus will transform us, our households, and our cultures in their entirety over a period of time as the gospel takes root.

Isaiah talks about these evangelists when he says, "How beautiful on the mountains are the feet of those who bring good news, who proclaim peace" (Isa. 52:7). Paul expounds further on this in Romans 10:14–15.

> How, then, can they call on the one they have not believed in? And how can they believe in the one of whom they have not heard? And how can they hear without someone preaching to them? And how can anyone preach unless they are sent? As it is written: How beautiful are the feet of those who bring good news!

We would not be believers today unless someone had proclaimed to us the gospel of Christ. Without evangelists, no new culture would hear the good news. They are commissioned by the Lord to lead the church into new places to extend the gospel so that all will hear. The evangelist is also responsible for training God's people to do that work within our own culture and network of relationships. Most of us will not get beyond talking to people who are just like us. We will probably not learn a new language or take on a different culture in order to share the gospel. But we do need training to learn to minister the gospel to other people—our families, friends, coworkers, neighbors—and God has given evangelists as a special gift to the church to lead us into that work of ministry.

Many of us are in local bodies situated in diverse neighborhoods with different language groups and cultures, and we are not reaching all the people around us. If we are going to be true to the mission of God, we need evangelists to mobilize us and lead us in the work of reaching our neighborhoods and cities for Christ.

PASTORS AND TEACHERS

The last two equipping gifts of pastors and teachers are to be taken together. Like the first three, they also have a ministry of the word, but theirs is with those who have come to believe in Christ. This shows a progression. First, the apostles and prophets carry on their ministries when there are few believers; they listen to the Lord and bring the Word of God to us. Then the evangelists come and introduce the gospel to people who have never before heard it, resulting in a population that believes—and now needs to be taught—the Word of the Lord. Finally, the pastors and teachers teach the Word in the body of Christ. This equipping will continue until that great and glorious day when we all will finally become like Jesus.

The Great Commission (see Matt. 28:19–20) tells us that the work of making disciples is not complete when people say, "I have decided to follow Jesus." The work of discipleship carries on throughout our lives until we learn to obey God in everything He has taught us. This is the work of pastors and teachers. How many of us in coming to Jesus, or even after forty years of being a believer, can say, "I know everything the Bible teaches"? We begin as babies in Christ and must be fed and nurtured if we are to grow to maturity in Christ.

Pastors and teachers are to be, as Peter says in First Peter 5:1–4, undershepherds of the flock of God. Jesus is the Great Shepherd the sheep, but He has assigned elders and pastors to be shepherds under Him to care for the sheep of God, to feed believers in the green pastures of God's Word. So the unique ministry of the pastors and teachers, as we are told in Acts 6:1–4, is the ministry of the Word and of prayer.

The pastoring and teaching gifts entail proclaiming the whole counsel of God worldwide, discipling believers in all that Christ commands. Pastors and teachers are assigned the responsibility for developing leadership within the church (see Titus 1:5–9). They are to feed the saints spiritually, pointing to Christ and leading the way within the congregation by word and example (see 1 Tim. 4:11–16). They are also to defend the faith against those who oppose Christ and attack the church. When we as saints get off track or wander away, just as sheep do from the fold, pastors and teachers are to correct and discipline us (see Acts 20:17–35).

THE RESULT: EVERY BELIEVER MATURING AND SERVING

God has given all the special equipping gifts to the body of Christ to prepare us for the work of ministry. That is critical so that we, as the people of God, are well-nourished on the Word and equipped to carry on our vital function of ministry in the body and into the world. The result of the equipping ministry is that every believer will mature to the fullness of life in Christ and serve for the growth of the body in one way or another. That growth to maturity will happen only as each one does its part: leaders leading, teachers teaching, members serving one with another "until we all reach unity in the faith and in the knowledge of the Son of God and become mature, attaining to the whole measure of the fullness of Christ" (Eph. 4:13).

Those with the five "word" gifts are all to equip the full body for its work of service. "Service" here translates to the Greek word for "deaconing." Yes, every member is to be a deacon, while this ministry of the whole body of Christ is coordinated by those filling the formal role of "deacon." That ensures God's ministry of care, justice, and mercy is carried out by the whole church for the blessing of all.

Only when every member takes up his or her part does the body grow. The Lord requires each of us to use our gifts in the work of ministry. Christ has given us the special gifts of apostles, prophets, evangelists, pastors, and teachers to equip and mobilize us until we all come to the fullness of Christ. That is the divine design for mobilizing the body for ministry. That is the reality that we are to strive for as the people of God. That is certainly what God is seeking to bring about in each local congregation of believers. And it is a reality that will certainly happen. It will be completed on that great and glorious day when Jesus Christ comes again. As John proclaims: "Dear friends, now we are children of God, and what we will be has not yet been made known. But we know that when Christ appears, we shall be like him, for we shall see him as he is" (1 John 3:2).

12

BUILDING RELATIONSHIPS
AND TRANSFORMING COMMUNITIES

S piritual maturity will naturally produce healthy relationships, both within the body of Christ and outside of it.
In seeking to minister Christ to the people we rub shoulders with every day, building relationships and partnerships will
be vital to the transformation of those who live around us and,
eventually, entire communities. But we have to seek these relationships out.

CREATING SYNERGISTIC PARTNERSHIPS IN THE
COMMUNITY

Every neighborhood is made up of living systems of people.[1]
We all realize that most people in a community belong to some
type of organization—a local church, a religious group, or a local club. If we expand our thinking, though, we will find that
people belong to a great diversity of groups. It could be a parent group whose children attend the same school, or a group

of people who all frequent the same clothing or grocery store. The group may be made up of car owners or of those who use public transit, or it could be defined by the employed or by stay-at-home parents. In a community, we want to identify all these groups and then figure out how to create synergistic partnerships with them. We can do more together than either group can do on its own, and these kinds of partnerships can help us promote the gospel as well as live out missions of mercy and justice among the people in our areas.

A great example of synergistic partnerships can be found in the Hunting Park section of north Philadelphia. There one can find about a dozen organizations working together for the sake of the gospel and the community. The most obvious is Esperanza Health Center, with around eighty staff on location and a beautiful new building on reclaimed land. Next to it is Joy in the City, a privately owned building that houses a range of for-profit and non-profit entities—including a Christian legal clinic; classrooms for Cairn University and Biblical Seminary; church-planting meeting spaces; Goodlands Construction; Vocatio Career Prep School; a bike shop called Simple Cycle; and the building owners, ServiceMaster, a cleaning company.

Across the street is Hunting Park Christian Academy, housed in Spirit and Truth Fellowship. Half a block from there is Ayuda Community Center, followed by Orange Korner Arts. It's a short walk from there to One Hope Community Church, 8th Street Community Church, Grace and Peace Community Church, and Hunting Park House Church—all highly engaged local congregations.

In densely populated urban communities in the United States, it isn't uncommon to find numerous churches in close proximity. People walked to church when most church build-ings were built, and attendance was normally much higher than it is today (although this does not necessarily mean that those attending were Christ followers). What stands out in Hunting Park is the synergistic partnership of these churches and organi-zations working together. Walking the block on an average day, one can see people from these groups interacting—sometimes formally, more often informally—whether it's the staff at the legal clinic having lunch at the health center's café, or a teach-er getting a part for his bike, or a church member mentoring a Vocatio student. Beautiful mosaics made by kids in the arts program at Orange Korner hang in the bike shop. Vocatio uses Simple Cycle's welding units and the health center gym. Some-times money changes hands, but more often each group contrib-utes whatever services or goods they can, where they can. It is a truly remarkable sight—these groups working together, sharing, loving, strategizing. Other communities may offer all these ser-vices, but most often they are led or "owned" by one group. In Hunting Park each group is autonomous, yet each one is com-mitted to the vision of taking the gospel to their community.

How does this kind of partnership come about? In this case, it began with a struggling older congregation having the courage to pretty much give away their building to a growing new church. Though the two churches were from different denominations and ethnic groups, they shared the common goal of furthering the gospel in their community. The older congregation, pastored by Doug Rogers, a dedicated collaborator for decades, saw that it could best continue its love for people by moving on. The new congregation, led by the visionary pastor Manny Ortiz, was able to honor the previous group and show a beautiful picture of hope.

Manny began with a small group of highly dedicated members and a heart for those in the community. As the church grew, he pushed all church attendees to find ways to engage and love their local community. Regardless of where church members lived, the location of the church was where the congregation would commit its resources. From one congregation grew numerous church plants, some in other parts of the city but four in Hunting Park. The church's belief was that its community was so diverse in how it functioned, no single congregation could fulfill the mission of reaching every man, woman, and child with the gospel.

As the church grew, so did its ethnic and economic diversity. The members were committed to building the community; and as they were encouraged to see God's vision, they were also empowered to create new works. This growing vision went far beyond the original church, as those who were not from that church began to hope that they could locate their own ministries in that synergistic collaboration. The original founders of that vision, like Manny Ortiz and Randy and Sue Baker, still walk alongside many of today's leaders, but they have had the humility to let things grow beyond themselves and create space for others to thrive.

BUILDING PARTNERSHIPS WITH OTHER CHURCHES

Not every community has a Manny Ortiz and a Doug Rogers to spark such a work; but if we look, we will find the same building blocks. God has placed His people throughout communities, and the Holy Spirit resides in those people. What could be more powerful than that?

Many efforts at collaboration fail, often because the person leading them believes that his or her ideas should be important to everyone else. This is similar to how many churches communicate that God is speaking to them in a vacuum, that the church's own vision is the most important thing for its community. Convincing the pastor of such a church to take a few hours out to meet with other pastors can be a chore, as he or she always has "so much to do." It takes significant investment in others to discover that we can do more together than we can alone.

So where to begin? First, we need to meet with as many other churches in our communities as possible and affirm that God is at work in them. This forms the basis for establishing cooperative partnerships. If we are willing to invest in others, we will find that most are willing to invest in us. Turning up at a special service for the pastor of another church, responding to an e-mail from another ministry leader in a timely way, inviting people out and simply listening to their hearts and stories are the beginnings of developing synergistic partnerships.

Next comes the humility to understand that while our work is important, so is the work of every child of God. We must affirm this, celebrate this, encourage this, and believe this. As we seek to reach out to others, we should value their time and interests. Gathering together for the sake of gathering together rarely works. Finding what others are passionate about and then connecting with them on those issues will produce far greater results.

When Common Grace holds a collaborative gathering, we don't try and get everyone we can to attend. We strategically invite each guest for a reason. We have already invested something in them, even if it is as small as attending their church or taking them to breakfast. We usually have an idea of their passions and strengths. If we want to talk about creating a thrift store in the community, we invite those who we know have that interest or we think can be shown the value in doing this to achieve their mission, not ours. If we want to talk about education, we look for people who have expressed a desire to do that work. We start small and build from there. This is different from the more typical approach of trying to get as many people together as possible, seeing who is interested, and then forming a group. That may work on rare occasions, but more often than not it sends a message that the person thinks everyone should join his or her idea.

When we start small and build, word gets out to the right people and they ask to join. And when people ask if they can join our collaboration, we already have buy-in. We don't have to expend time and energy (ours or theirs) convincing them of anything. We love it when this happens.

Being clear on purpose is important, but even more important is building relationships. We love hosting barbecues because they create an atmosphere in which people can gather and get to know one another. If we are the catalyst for a gathering, most people will know us but they may not know each other. We need to create the space for that. We don't want to be the focal point of things because then we limit the synergy that can take place. Connecting shouldn't be like a hub, with us or our organization at the center. Great connecting is like a web of interworking pieces. If people meet because of a particular person and go on to do amazing things together without that person, then he or she probably has the "gift" of being a connector. Synergistic partnerships have multiple dimensions. Remember, we aren't about building our own tribes—we are about building the Kingdom.

When Christian groups get together and begin by trying to come up with a common statement of faith, the road ahead will be a hard one. Focusing on a felt need initially is far easier and more inclusive. Many of Common Grace's partners, who we love and work with regularly, pastor churches where I (Coz) would struggle to be a member. That's just fine. Our collaboration isn't focused on a combined worship service or agreement on baptism; it's focused on a mutual desire to see the gospel furthered and a belief in a really big God who works through His people in all their diversity.

BUILDING PARTNERSHIPS IN OUR COMMUNITIES

Churches alone will not bring community transformation in complex systems, and collaborations should extend beyond them. Our partnerships need to include schools, businesses, secular nonprofits, and civil servants, among others.

Once again, we need to invest time in others and learn their goals and desires. If we are working on a collaboration around caring for children in our community, we will want the local school engaged, as well as the city government's child welfare division. This doesn't mean they need to come to every meeting or even have any significant stake in what we are doing, but we would want the largest provider of education to be part of the conversation. Common Grace has found consistently that through God's providence and common grace, these organizations have people within them who know and love God and may not have been engaged by the church already.

At a recent listening group that I (Coz) coordinated for Cairn University—a gathering of multiple groups for the university to hear what others thought they should be working on—we had representatives from public schools, private schools, charter schools, vocational schools, a Christian university, and a secular university. The conversation was rich as members of each group offered thoughts on a common goal of positive community transformation. Plenty of work had been done before the meeting so people would know that this would be worth their time—and good food never hurts turnout either. More than that, people wanted to help one another. To hear a public school principal bring a challenge and hear that challenge affirmed by a Christian school principal was a powerful thing.

We gave time before and after the meeting so people could get to know a little about each other, see who they knew in common, and exchange business cards. During the meeting, each person was given an opportunity to speak, and questions were directed in such a way as to make each person feel valued. Doing this wasn't hard when we knew that every person invited had a deep desire to see kids in our community receive quality education. Each group differed on how they thought that education was best delivered, but what we emphasized was the common thread.

INVESTING IN OUR PARTNERS

Once we have invested time in forming synergistic partnerships, we need to continue to invest in our partners. At Common Grace, we don't just call people when we need something or want them to be part of something. We constantly reach out to let people know they are valuable for who they are, not what they can do for us. A short phone call, e-mail, or text to let people know we are praying for them, that we read their latest newsletter, that we thought of them this past Sunday as they were delivering the Word, or on Monday when we knew they had a tough meeting at work, can go a long way toward maintaining and growing relationships. It is the simple things that show how we value others and God's work in them. Yes, this takes time but we can commit that time if we believe that we can do more together than we can apart.

A certain group of business people has invested significant resources into some ministries with whom Common Grace partners. We don't get any kickback from this, just the benefit of helping great people find ways to partner with other great people. These business people had visited our community numerous times to see God's work and had affirmed that work, so I (Coz) decided that the least I could do was visit their work about an hour away from our community.

I contacted them and asked if I could visit. "Are you sure you want to do that?" replied John. "You know what we do, right?"

"Yes, John, I'm sure. You've visited me a number of times and it's meant a lot to me. Let me return the favor."

"Okay," he said. "I'll bring you on the family tour, a special visit we usually reserve for family owners of the company. But don't say I didn't warn you."

When I arrived at their company headquarters, John once again gave me the option of backing out. *How bad could this be?* I silently wondered. As I entered the first room of the pig slaughterhouse, I quickly realized just how bad. John's family is one of the largest producers of pork products in the region. He must have thought the whole thing was much funnier than I did at that point. But at the end of the day, John walked away knowing that I valued him, his family, and their work above my own stomach. We remain friends and he continues to be a great advocate for our community.

REACHING ONE, TOUCHING MANY

Every one of us has relationships outside the church—family members, friends, coworkers, team members. Many people, however, see only a small subsection of their daily encounters with these people as opportunities to bring the gospel to the world. But when we understand how reaching just one person for Christ carries with it the potential to reach many others, we begin to see a whole new world of opportunities. This is an idea that we like to call "creating ripples in the pond."

Common Grace recently took students to a busy intersection in Kensington. As we walked the few blocks around the El, we passed hundreds of people. We had asked the students to survey people regarding access to health services, but first we wanted them to understand just how many different people groups crossed that intersection each day. There were the obvious ones: people coming to shop, people catching the train to work, people changing from a bus to a train. There were shop employees, business security guards, transit workers. We identified the parking authority worker (giving out tickets), police officers, the mail carrier, the water meter reader, garbage collectors, firefighters, city inspectors. A little more intimidating were the illegal drug dealers, their clients, those in prostitution, and the homeless. All these groups interact in that one intersection throughout the day. Some would see this as a great opportunity to hand out tracts or publicly proclaim the gospel, but we wanted our students to understand something different that day: Each of the people they saw knew other people; and if they reached just one person, that person could impact others in his or her circle of relationships and potentially bring many more to Christ.

Parents who send children to school have a built-in mechanism to facilitate relationships with others; and parents who homeschool are most likely part of a cooperative of some type, which creates another opportunity. The hope is that the cooperative is open to new people, especially those who don't yet know Jesus. What an opening!

If we spend any time each week buying groceries, we are again involved in a communal activity with the chance to interact with people—other shoppers, store employees, and even others we bring along to shop with us. This is one reason we should consider shopping locally, even if our choices are not as good as in other stores. We shouldn't be concerned just about getting the best food or great deals, but about effectively using our time and routines to build relationships.

A common idea in fitness for busy people is lifestyle activity or building exercise into one's daily routine. This might mean taking the stairs instead of the elevator, parking farther from the store, getting off the bus one stop earlier to walk extra steps. These simple things can build activity into our day without it feeling programmed. We can use exactly the same principle in order to create ripples in the pond. Integrating the intentional building of relationships with people into our everyday lives creates an effect that will expand ever outward.

In a large Asian city, I (Bill) tasked a group of urban pastors with figuring out strategies to share the gospel across a wide range of people. One strategy focused on how to reach taxi drivers.

The pastors calculated how many encounters those drivers had across the city and how diverse those encounters were for each driver. Based on this, they figured if they could reach the drivers, they could reach the city as the drivers interacted with customers. The problem was that most drivers worked long hours and didn't have time to join a Sunday morning gathering. In fact, they had little time for anything outside of their taxi driving. So these pastors came up with the idea of taxi rest stops, a place where a driver could pull in and get a hot meal while someone cleaned out his vehicle and washed it. While the driver ate, those who staffed the rest stops would have the opportunity to talk with the driver. Reach the driver, reach the city.

"Uber evangelism" is a term I (Coz) first heard used by a local pastor who chose to become an Uber driver in his neighborhood. "The opportunity to meet people I otherwise would never encounter was too good to pass up," he told me. Driving also helped supplement his meager church salary. Ripples in the pond.

"Reaching one, touching many" is a great way for a network of churches to think about how they can reach their local neighborhoods through natural relationships. It is also how a church becomes part of a neighborhood rather than just a regional place of gathering. Calvary Church in Montgomery County, Pennsylvania, is a large church and can easily appear to be using an attractional model of ministry. But delve deeper and one can see that they are working toward using relational encounters in an east coast suburb, a context where it can be difficult to develop a sense of community.

When Calvary began looking at new strategies to reach its community through ongoing relationships, its leadership began

asking, "How does our community interact?" After they observed children's sports, stay-at-home mothers, birthday parties,
and school events, they put a coffee shop and a children's playground in their church with the stipulation that it would be
used for community events, not church events. Next they built
high-quality sports fields, again for the community.

One of their more interesting additions was an annual sports
expo—focused on hunting and fishing, for the most part—in
an attempt to meet more men from the area. This expo now
brings more than ten thousand men through the church doors
whenever it is held.

Not everyone has all the resources of a Calvary to build a coffee shop or soccer field, but we can all find natural connecting
points for people in our areas. Reaching one will create ripples
in the pond and lead to reaching many.

TRANSFORMING WHOLE COMMUNITIES

If reaching one person carries with it the potential to reach
many, then entire communities can be transformed. But this will
take understanding our local neighborhoods, being in partnership with other ministries, and unleashing our churches to create ripples in the pond.

People are most effective when they build natural relationships
in their natural contexts. This idea has been covered extensively
by authors over the past fifty years, sometimes to great effect,
although other times as a way of maintaining the racially and
ethnically exclusionary thinking that the recent Western church
has exhibited. But if we create natural relationships around us
and follow the ripples they create throughout a neighborhood

and community, we may be surprised at just how much diversity exists around us. Bryan Loritts in *Letters to a Birmingham Jail* and Dr. Soong-Chan Rah in *The Next Evangelicalism* both make strong arguments that the church remains one of the most segregated groups in all American society. Employment, schooling, transit, and housing all show far less segregation than churches do. If believers created and followed the natural relationships in their everyday lives, the church could well take a step toward becoming less segregated.

Don Graves, a Philadelphia-based church planter, describes the phenomenon of people being separated from their natural relationships after they become Christians. He talks about two islands—Saved Island and Unsaved Island. (I often wonder if he was watching the TV show *Survivor* as he pondered this.) He says that the church likes to exist on Saved Island. It is our cultural comfort zone for gathering. When we're together, we send out missionaries to Unsaved Island. Sometimes they reach people with the gospel and they quickly try to drag those people back to live on Saved Island. But in doing this, they often disconnect those people from many of their existing relationships. We often think this is a good idea if former relationships were bad influences on people—after all, these new creations in Christ should live new lives.

But this model creates a strategy of individualistic evangelism—reaching one person at a time, usually in isolation from others. If instead we were to set up a support system on Unsaved Island and encourage new believers to maintain their familiar relationships in their cultural context, we could create a people movement where believers are more likely to be effective. Jesus put it a little more harshly than Don does: "Woe to you, teachers of the law and Pharisees, you hypocrites! You travel over land and sea to win a single convert, and when you have succeeded, you make them twice as much a child of hell as you are" (Matt. 23:15). Jesus was referring to the idea of taking someone out of his or her cultural context and making that person a slave to the law. We need to be careful not to follow the same patterns the Pharisees did.

Common Grace has seen a similar situation around the world as missionaries build compounds to try to reach local communities. There, those missionaries often replicate their own native culture. The compounds may not actually be gated communities, though they often can be; they may simply be a network of so-called like-minded people who live in housing that reflects where they came from, send their children to missionary schools, and congregate and worship with others most like them. Then they tell their supporters back home how difficult the work is, how long it takes to make an impact and see change take place.

Yes, it does take a long time to enculturate another person, but that has never been the mission of the church. Our mission is to go and make disciples of Christ, not disciples of our cultures. A community of believers truly integrated into its neighborhood will see far greater results than those produced by a compound mentality. If we were to spend all our lives trying to create the perfect Christian community for our family and friends, would it be any surprise if we were not effective in making new disciples? Are our churches part of a neighborhood, integrated into the life fabric of the area, or just social clubs for those who look and act like us?

13

WHEN DISCRIMINATION HINDERS MERCY MINISTRY

I n Acts 6:1–7, we learn that the early church in Jerusalem was growing rapidly. When the Spirit first came upon the church (see Acts 2), there were about 120 believers who had gathered in that upper room on the day of Pentecost. After the Spirit was poured out, the Word of God went forth with great power and the Lord added quickly many thousands of people to the church. On the day of Pentecost alone, about three thousand were added (see 2:41). With a growing church committed to God's work of ministry through teaching, service, and witnessing, there also came problems. In Acts 6, we have a picture of a rapidly growing church encountering difficulties, but the Lord gave His solution for the mobilization of the body.

This church is not unlike our own. As we carry out the work of the ministry in our communities, we can expect difficulties. We can expect opposition. We can expect our own sin to get in the way. In the midst of these challenges, we need to look to the Lord to remove our sin so His Spirit's work might flourish in our midst.

DISCRIMINATION IN THE EARLY CHURCH

In Acts 6, we read that the church had adopted the Old Testament practice of caring for their widows. The Lord had commanded Israel to take special care of the poor, the stranger, the alien, the widow, and the orphan (see Deut. 10:17–19). The Lord called upon Israel to embrace these people and bring them into the family of God so they might experience His grace in word and deed.

The Lord similarly challenged the church early on. He had called the body to be a people who lived out of the grace of God. They were engaged in the ministry of deliverance, in which people were set free from earthly bondage into the glorious liberty of the children of God. Part of that glorious liberty meant being embraced, welcomed, and incorporated into the family of God.

The early church had a special life in which believers spent quality time together. They were not just together on Sundays in the Lord's house, but they spent time with each other in their homes. They also shared what they respectively had so that no one lacked (see Acts 2:41–47). All this is a picture of jubilee as it is outlined in Leviticus 25:8–55, in Isaiah 61, and in Jesus' own announcement in Luke 4:14–21. In Jesus' ministry of healing and bringing liberty to people who were captive to sin and the oppressive forces around them, the early church saw a demonstration of the practice of jubilee. But as the early church practiced this, they also experienced difficulty.

In Acts 6, we have the account of a great dissension that came into their midst when one part of the body, the Hellenistic Jews, charged the Hebraic or Jerusalem Jews with discrimination in the way food was distributed to their widows. It was the responsibility of the body to care for the fatherless and the widowed, and part of that was to provide for their daily sustenance of food. So the church brought tithes of their food to the body of Christ so it could be distributed to those in need. Apparently, in that distribution, some folks got preference over others and that led to division in the body. The church had to deal with it.

Another example of discrimination facing the early church was when the church had great difficulty accepting God's call to carry the gospel to the Gentiles. The Jewish believers found it difficult to believe that the Holy Spirit had really come upon the Gentiles and that God intended Gentiles to be incorporated into His family. God had to instruct the church about His saving purposes to the Jews first and also to the Gentiles (see Rom. 1:16; 2:9–10).

The gospel has come to break down the walls that divide us. Whoever calls upon the name of the Lord, whether Jew or Gentile, free or slave, rich or poor, becomes a child of God. Each one has equal standing and status before the Lord and indeed among each other.

STRONG WORDS AGAINST DISCRIMINATION

In James 2:1–13, James had to speak strongly to the church struggling with discrimination in the body of Christ. Verse 9 succinctly captures his point: "If you show favoritism, you sin and are convicted by the law as lawbreakers."

There is no place in the body of Christ for discrimination among the saints. There is no Jew or Gentile, rich or poor, bond or free, black or white. We are all one in Christ. We are to seek the interests of others more highly than we seek our own.

The apostles had to address the crisis of discrimination that had come into the body of Christ with a sense of grief and shame.

We face similar challenges in our own day. It is important for us to visit this passage in Acts 6 because it shows striking parallels between the discrimination the early church faced and the discrimination we face today. We need to understand God's call to us if we are to understand His work of ministry among us and how He wants us to carry on His work.

WHY CARE ABOUT THE MINISTRY OF MERCY?

The problem of discrimination caused great dissension in the church. Perhaps some shouting went on. Animosity took deep root in the life of the church because of the favoritism being shown. It would have been easy for the apostles, in the midst of all the work they had to do at that time (given the large numbers who were rapidly coming to Christ) to say, "Who needs the hassle of this ministry? Let's just stop distributing food to the widows. Let them take care of themselves or let their families take care of them. What does it have to do with us, the family of God?"

It is interesting, looking at Acts 6, that this option was not even considered. We do not find the apostles engaging in the thought, even for a moment, that mercy ministry should be dropped in spite of the many hassles it involved. Why? After all, if the work was causing that much trouble, who needed it? A number of passages, both in the Old and New Testaments, show us why putting a pause on mercy ministry was not a consideration in the early church.

Deuteronomy 10:12–21. In this passage the writer says very simply, "Israel—church—remember where God met you."

God met us when we were strangers and aliens to His family, when we were strangers and aliens to God Himself, when we were without hope because we were without God in the world. We were family-less. We were homeless. We were landless. When we were strangers, aliens in a foreign land, God chose to visit us with His mercy. It was there that the Lord embraced us, took up our causes, and defended us. With His outstretched arms, He delivered each of us out of our own personal "Egypt" and took us to that land that was ours not by right, but by mercy. Remember where God met us in mercy. As a people of God's merciful choice, showered with His lavish love, we are to join God in His ministry to the discarded, the broken, and the downtrodden of the world because there God chooses to shine His love and grace.

Psalm 68:5–6. In this passage, we are told that God, in His holy dwelling, is a "father to the fatherless, a defender of widows." God sets the lonely in families. He leads forth the prisoners with singing, but the rebellious live in a sun-scorched land. God's strategy for the broken of the world—the downtrodden, the discarded, the all alone, the stranger, the alien, the homeless, and the street wanderer—is that they be put into families. By virtue of our faith in Christ, we are members of the most glorious clan that ever existed. God has made for us, through this family, a big home with a big heart and lots of space to include others like ourselves who are strangers and aliens and broken and downtrodden in the world. God placed the lonely in families to take care of their family needs.

If a widow or a fatherless child had no provision for daily bread, it was the ministry of Israel—and later the church—to extend the mercy of God by providing that person with food and clothing. Israel was to be the widow's and the orphan's defender before an accusing and oppressive world.

The Bible is filled with references regarding widows and orphans. Because they had no defender in court, they could not plead their case. Boundaries were marked out around a person's land by stones placed at the corners of the lot; and in the dark of night, a defenseless widow sometimes had a neighbor who moved those stones a bit at a time, taking from her the land that was hers. Because she had no voice in the law courts, she was defenseless. God's people, who loved mercy and sought justice, were to make sure that the widowed and the fatherless were not exploited by the oppressors around them (see Prov. 15:25).

Deuteronomy 14:28–29. This scripture tells us how the Lord provided for the widow's needs.

> At the end of every three years, bring all the tithes of that year's produce and store it in your towns, so that the Levites (who have no allotment or inheritance of their own) and the foreigners, the fatherless and the widows who live in your towns may come and eat and be satisfied, and so that the Lord your God may bless you in all the work of your hands.

When Israel brought a tithe of that which they had produced to the house of the Lord, it was to be used to care for those who ministered there. But it was also to care for the aliens, the widows, and the fatherless who were landless and had no means of growing their own food. It was Israel's way of providing for their needs. Those who had were to take their tithe and give to those who did not have. It was the law of the Lord.

Ezekiel 22:6–12. The reason the judgment of the Lord came upon Israel, so that they ultimately lost control of their own land and were exiled, was that they had not practiced justice and sought mercy. In Ezekiel 22, we see the judgment of the Lord upon Israel for their sin. Here are His words in part: "In you they have treated father and mother with contempt; in you they have oppressed the foreigner and mistreated the fatherless and the widow. . . . In you are people who accept bribes to shed blood; you take interest and make a profit from the poor. You extort unjust gain from your neighbors. And you have forgotten me, declares the Sovereign LORD" (22:7, 12).

These are strong words. Israel had forgotten that they had experienced the Lord's mercy and were not returning it in practice. So the Lord withdrew His hand from them and allowed the surrounding oppressive nations to overrun them and take them into captivity. In exile, they had lots of time to think about the injustice they had practiced.

Micah 6:8. There was one sacrifice that most pleased the Lord. It wasn't the sacrifice of the animals in the temple brought to be offered on the altar. Rather, it was what Micah wrote of: "He has shown you, O mortal, what is good. / And what does the LORD require of you? / To act justly and to love mercy / and to walk humbly with your God."

James 1:27. James wrote that "religion that God our Father accepts as pure and faultless is this: to look after orphans and widows in their distress and to keep oneself from being polluted by the world." This passage is more accurately translated, "Pure and undefiled religion is this: to bring deliverance to the widow and the fatherless in their oppression and to keep yourselves unstained from the world." James was talking about the very thing the Old Testament taught. If we are a people who understand God's mercy in our lives, we will be a people who practice mercy with those the world is trampling under its feet. They are the very apple of God's eye: the poor, the widowed, the fatherless, the stranger, the alien, the homeless, the wanderers among us.

First Timothy 5:3–16. In this chapter, Paul instructs the church about the widows. His words are consistent with the teaching of the Old Testament about Israel's role in caring for its widows. In verse 4, we are told that it is first of all a family's responsibility to take care of a widow. If we are the children of a widow, it is our responsibility to make provision for her. If the widow is a younger woman who desires to be remarried, it is the family's responsibility to see to it that she is; consequently, she will be put into a family where her needs can be met. But if a widow has no family to care for her and is not young enough to remarry and have children of her own, it is the obligation of the church to take care of her. She is a widow indeed.

A widow indeed is more than sixty years old, has been faithful to her husband, and has been "well known for her good deeds, such as bringing up children, showing hospitality, washing the feet of the Lord's people," and "helping those in trouble" (5:9–10). Those who are widows indeed are to be cared for in the community of the church with the daily distribution of food, clothing, and shelter and defended in a court of law if necessary.

We can see from Scripture that it was not an option for the church in Acts 6 to say, "Too big a hassle! We can't take this one on. We have more important things to do." What is more important than the demonstration of the grace and the mercy of the Lord in a world that is cruel and hard and discarding?

WRONG SOLUTION—LEAVE IT TO THE LEADERS

In our Acts 6 text, it is interesting that the preferred solution for those who came to the apostles about this matter seemed to be to let the apostles take care of it. After all, it was the apostles' job to oversee the body of Christ. It seemed logical that these men with the greatest wisdom, theologically astute and well-versed in the Scriptures, would be the ones to handle the issue. But the apostles recognized that such a solution would not be wise. They knew that the mercy ministry must continue, but it was not a job for one or two. It was the ministry of the whole body.

More good things from the Lord have been ruined by taking the responsibility from the body and giving it to a few. The body sits and watches and says, "Well, thank God that somebody cares about this so I won't have to get involved." But the Lord's way of doing mercy ministry is to say, "This ministry is not the responsibility of a few who are especially endowed with grace. Rather it is the responsibility of the entire body."

The apostles knew that if they took up the ministry of mercy, they would be diverted from God's assignment to exercise the Word and pray on behalf of the congregation. Without spiritual food for the body, there would be one issue after another of its kind because the church would not be fed and nourished in the instruction of the Lord. Without the apostles' devotion to the ministry of prayer, the church would not be defended before the throne of grace from the vultures who would take advantage of the body through false teaching and spiritual attack. It would be a disaster if the apostles left their ministry to take up what was the whole body's ministry.

CORRECT SOLUTION—COORDINATE GOD'S PEOPLE TO SERVE

Instead, the apostles had another idea. They told the believers, "Choose seven men from among you who are known to be full of the Spirit and wisdom. We will turn this responsibility over to them and will give our attention to prayer and the ministry of the word" (Acts 6:3–4).

It is important for us to understand one key concept here. When we read, "We will turn this responsibility over to them," many of us might think, *Good! God gave the job to seven men, so everyone else is free from this awful burden.* But the passage should more accurately read, "Appoint seven we may put in charge of this task" or "appoint seven who will coordinate this task." These seven would have the wisdom to work through all of the division to unite the body, helping the believers to understand their place of service so that everybody could rise to the occasion, take their part, and make the work light. These seven were not apt to wait on the tables and distribute the food day after day after day. Rather, they were put in charge of straightening out the mess and coordinating the tasks so that the body would function as it should.

Something like this indeed took place because in the very next chapters, two of those seven were doing something entirely different. Philip was out on the road communicating the gospel to the Ethiopian eunuch, leading him to Christ, baptizing him in the name of the triune God, and incorporating him into the body of Christ. And Stephen was in front of the Jewish rulers, on trial, about to be executed for proclaiming the gospel in word. Either these two were irresponsible and had abandoned their task or what they had been assigned to do was of an administrative nature. I would contend that what they were assigned to do was set in order that which was broken, so that the body as a whole would function together in the work of the ministry.

Some people believe that this passage is the beginning of the office of the deacon. Many who look at it this way have narrow vision. They say the work of the diaconate is the work of mercy in the body of Christ. As I study the Old and New Testaments, I believe that this passage teaches that the work of mercy in the body of Christ is the ministry of each and every believer. It is the very mark of the redeemed children of God to be a people of mercy who seek justice. No one is exempt. None of us is free to practice discrimination, to avoid the needs in the world in which we live. Mercy ministry is everyone's responsibility.

SPIRITUAL QUALIFICATIONS FOR DEACONS

If this work of ministry is going to be done, a work of co-ordination and a ministry of judgment are needed in the body because there is so much to do.

It is interesting that the sole qualifications were being full of the Spirit and having wisdom. The Old Testament parallel is found in Exodus 18:13–16, where we read that Moses almost immediately got taken up with the work of settling disputes among the children of Israel in the wilderness. He spent all day sitting in judgment on the cases that came his way. His wise father-in-law, Jethro, came to him and said, "Moses, if you keep doing this, the line will only get longer, and you will sit here a long time, because the problems will multiply." Jethro understood that the congregation of God's people were sinners saved

204 | PLACE MATTERS

by grace. There would be problems of sin in their midst, and they would need help to put an end to their sinful practices so they could exercise righteousness. God's people needed wise leaders to settle the divisions among them with justice and mercy if they were going to be coordinated in the ministry. Jethro instructed Moses that he needed a whole army of people to handle the problem. He needed elders who would be in charge of hundreds and fifties and tens so that he would have to consider only the hard cases. Moses was encouraged to enlist wise men who could be put in charge of settling disputes (see Exod. 18:17–23).

The work of the diaconate is first and foremost a ministry of judgment or justice, a ministry of wisdom in coordinating the body of Christ so that God's people can all work together in the ministry the Lord has assigned us. Praise God that He gives those gifts to His body. Praise God that He gives teachers who devote themselves to the ministry of the Word and prayer. Praise God that He gives people full of the Spirit and wisdom to coordinate us that we might minister the mercy and justice of the Lord.

People from many different nations of the earth have no gospel witness today. Many people are broken and downtrodden; many homes are fatherless; many older women have no defender at their side. The Lord says to us, "Church, love mercy and seek justice. Embrace the stranger and the alien, the widow and the fatherless, with the mercy of the Lord. Place them into your families so that in your midst they might experience the love and mercy of the Savior." God has called each and every local congregation to participate in this ministry of mercy. May He grant us a willingness to rise up and be His people in this way for Jesus' sake!

14

LIFE TOGETHER—A CALL TO CHRISTIAN COMMUNITY

Every one of us, as we have seen, is a minister in the body of Christ for the growth of one another. God has given spiritual gifts to each one of us to extend His grace to others so that they too may know Him. In essence, this is a call to life together—Christian community.

This is the very ministry that Jesus Himself carried out, intended to bring jubilee to our neighborhoods (see Lev. 25:8–55). The jubilee community proclaims the gospel message to those around us—a message of good news to the poor, the broken, the strangers and aliens that Jesus receives sinners. It is also a ministry of deliverance for people who are in bondage. As we minister to each other, we are able to bring relief to those who are captive to sin of all kinds. We can bring restoration to fellowship with the Lord and restoration of fellowship with each other.

When we live in joyful community, it not only benefits us as believers but also represents the body of Christ as it is meant to be for those living in our neighborhoods, and draws them to this kind of glad relationship. Indeed, we are called to gather people together into the family of God where we share the riches of His grace with them.

FELLOWSHIP IN THE EARLY CHURCH

One of the things we know from Acts 2 is that the people who met together on the day of Pentecost were strangers to each other. In fact, in many cases in the early church, the believers were strangers and aliens—Gentiles. But as the Lord began to build His church, He crossed barriers and called Gentiles as well as Jews into His family so that those who were formerly alienated from one another became friends together in Christ. This is a picture of life at every level. The new believers met daily in the temple courts (see 2:46) for worship. They needed to be together every day because of the opposition against them.

The new believers also "ate together with glad and sincere hearts" in their homes (2:46). They shared Christ with one another around the table, even though the ridicule and persecution against the early church were great. They were a new people. They were family together.

They also shared their goods with one another. In Acts 2:44–45, we read, "All the believers were together and had everything in common. They sold property and possessions to give to anyone who had need." They began to practice the great Christian grace of recognizing that in life together, all that we are and have comes from the Lord. Nothing we have belongs to us alone. What one has is for someone else, if that person has a need greater than the first. So the early Christians were a generous people, willing to give up what they had for the benefit of others in the family.

They sold their goods and gave to one another according to their needs so that there might be equality (see 2 Cor. 8:1–15). There was an outpouring of generous and lavish love toward one another as they daily shared their lives.

We cannot do this if we don't spend time together and know each other deeply. But one of the great challenges in the church today is that we lead busy lives fragmented from one another. Sometimes the only time we see each other is at eleven on a Sunday morning. There we appear in our finest veneer with hair done, makeup on, and clothes pressed. We look as if all is well. But when we spend life together in the family, we know that sometimes not everything is as it looks. We see each other in our ugliness, pain, heartache, troubles, and trials. As we see each other's needs clearly, we recognize that as brothers and sisters in the Lord, we are to share what we have so that others might be lifted up.

How do we share our lives? Are we bringing our lives together into family, meeting together not just on Sundays but finding significant times with each other in more natural settings? We can do this in our homes or as we walk along the way. We can do it in our workplaces and in those places where we are carrying out our calling before the Lord.

We must not think that we are getting all Jesus has to offer if all we do is get together with the saints in the worship service on Sunday. We are not even getting it all if we belong to a small group. We need to be finding ways at all levels of life to be spending time with our family members in Jesus. In this time and age when people are so mobile, we must work doubly hard at it.

FOUR DIMENSIONS OF LIFE TOGETHER

As we spend time together, it must not be only in general fun, but in a deep level of ministry with one another as well. Look at Acts 2:42: "They devoted themselves (or they continually devoted themselves together) to the apostles' teaching and to fellowship, to the breaking of bread and to prayer." The four dimensions shown us in this verse give us a fuller picture of what life together in Jesus encompasses. We are to continually devote ourselves *together* to these things, not just personally or individually. The passage is talking about our life together in the Lord, one believer with another. It is in our life together that we benefit from what God is doing for each of us in these areas.

The apostles' teaching. In our lives together, we are to begin our fellowship with an open Bible, devoting ourselves to the study of the apostles' teaching. The apostles' teaching is "useful for teaching, rebuking (showing us what is wrong), correcting (telling us the right way to go instead) and training in righteousness, so that the servant of God may be thoroughly equipped for every good work" (2 Tim. 3:16–17). We learn this together as we examine the Scriptures corporately.

None of us know everything in the Bible. I daresay that even if all of us were to put our collective knowledge of the Bible together, we still would not have a complete knowledge of the Word of God. We need the teaching ministry of one another if we are to gain full and complete insight into what God is saying in His Word and apply it to our lives.

As we gather together in fellowship, it should not be an intrusion to our time together to have the Bible open. It should be natural to our lives together. As we hear one another express different needs, we should be able to open the Word of God and search it together to find God's answers.

Fellowship. In the American church today, we have trivialized fellowship. We are to be devoted to it. Fellowship is with God's Son, Jesus Christ, and with one another. It is a fellowship of learning God's forgiveness for our sins and ministering God's grace, one with another. It is a fellowship in Christ's suffering. It is a fellowship in Christ's grace. So when we come together around the apostles' teaching, it is not just the apostles ministering Christ's Word to us, it is also a fellowship in which we minister the Word to one another as well, sharing the lessons God is teaching us in our lives.

When one person says, "God is doing something in my life and I'm not sure what He is up to," we can come together in a fellowship of ministry that searches God's Word to find out "what's up" from God's perspective. It is a fellowship on the deepest level. It is Jesus' ministry in the body. God has given each of us gifts for ministry, and we received those gifts through His ministry in our own lives. As God showered His grace on us in our brokenness and brought healing to us, He was also equipping us for ministry to others. It is from that base of God's dealing in our lives that we fellowship with one another around the Word and pass on what Jesus has given us.

Breaking of bread. We are also to be devoted to the breaking of bread. In the early Christian church, it was an observance, almost on a daily basis, of communion. In the breaking of bread, we remember the benefits of the cross until Jesus comes. As we receive God's grace in our lives in this way, we are continually reminded by the Lord of how we stand in need of grace and, even more so, of the sufficiency of that grace to meet every need we have. Daily, as we encounter sin in our lives, the Lord comes to us in the breaking of bread and says, "Remember My body broken for you. Remember My blood shed for you. It is enough" (see 1 Cor. 11:24–25).

People living life together need Jesus to be present in the body with His abiding promise of forgiveness. If we don't have that, we quickly fall into the trap of thinking of ourselves as self-righteous, as righteous apart from the grace of God. But when we come together at this level of life, we see again and again our need of the work of Jesus on the cross and in the resurrection. Again and again, we must look to the cross. In the breaking of bread and the drinking of the cup, the saints of God taste and see that the Lord is good.

Prayer. Living our lives together also works itself out in prayer. This is not prayer in the general sense, but rather concrete prayer for one another in our deepest needs. As we come to know each other, we will know each other's needs. Based on the promises of God, our Father will hear whatever we ask in Jesus' name and answer according to His good and perfect will. His responses will continually surprise us.

We have a powerful instance of answered prayer in Acts 12:5–17, where we find the saints of God gathered together behind locked doors, praying for the release of Peter, who was in jail. They were asking the right thing of the right One in faith, but they didn't really expect God to grant their request. When a knock came on the door and Peter stood there, they fell back in surprise. Whoa, God had done it! This gave the believers a great sense of wonder and awe before the Lord. Indeed, the One who is at work in us is greater than he who is in the world.

LIFE TOGETHER LEADS TO PRAISE AND AWE OF GOD

We see, finally, the great impact this life together had on the believers and on the community: "Everyone was filled with awe at the many wonders and signs performed by the apostles" (Acts 2:43). What does this mean? It means that they were so surprised by the working of God that they were speechless.

We learn God's powerful working one day at a time, one event at a time, as it is evidenced in our lives together. This is why our testimonies are important; because as we share what God is doing in our lives and share our needs with each other, we will see that God is the same today as He was yesterday and that He will be faithful tomorrow also. He will surprise us to the point that all we can do is stand there with our mouths hanging wide open and say, "Wow! God is deep."

There is a difference between awe and praise. Praise comes out of awe. We are told in Acts 2:46–47 that as the believers "ate together with glad and sincere hearts," they were praising God. Praise came after they had seen the hand of God. If all we do is praise God for what He used to do, our praise will be feeble. But if we praise Him out of a sense of His faithfulness in the past, expecting Him to work again today, and we see His hand of recreating among us, we will be moved over and over again toward whole-souled praise to the Lord. It will be ecstatic praise, praise with our hands and feet and voices. We will be a *praise-full* people. Our sadness will be turned to joy.

LIFE TOGETHER HAS GREAT IMPACT ON OUR COMMUNITIES

This life together doesn't affect just us; it also has a life-changing impact on the world around us. Acts 2:47 says that the believers were "praising God and enjoying the favor of all the people." Luke is not talking about believers enjoying the favor of one another. He is talking about the unbelieving world around the church hearing their words of praise, receiving them with favor, and asking them to tell them about the hope that was in them (see 1 Pet. 3:15–16). When we praise God together, the world will want what we have.

As I (Bill) have studied Acts 2 over the years, I have asked, "When are the believers ever going to reach out?" It seems that all the things mentioned in this passage are inwardly directed into official church activities. But not so! Life together involves twenty-four hours of seven days of every week. It involves worshiping together in the corporate body; it also includes walking down the street, living in our homes, talking over the fence, sharing with our coworkers. It is the very substance of our lives. If we capture the picture that is presented here in Acts, we will be a people who are a light on top of a hill. We will be doing as the Lord said: "Let your light shine before others, that they may see your good deeds and glorify your Father in heaven" (Matt. 5:16).

That light will draw people to the Savior. That is what was happening in our passage. When the Christians shared their lives, they didn't do so just with believers. Paul says that we are to love one another deeply, especially those of the household of faith (see 1 Pet. 1:22; Gal. 6:10), but not only those of the household of faith. We are also to love those around us deeply—just as Jesus loved us. Jesus did not meet most of us at church. He met us on the street in our brokenness. He went to where we were. He did not ask us to come where He was. As we carry out this ministry of life together, we can embrace those who are yet outside relationship with Jesus in order to bring them in. That is what He did: "The Lord added to their number daily those who were being saved" (Acts 2:47).

LIFE TOGETHER IS A WITNESS TO THE RESURRECTED CHRIST

Witness in our communities doesn't just involve verbal communication of the gospel. It also involves life communication of the gospel. But as we share life with other believers, we are enabled also to share words with the unbelievers around us. Indeed, people will ask us for the hope that is within us and we will be able to tell them about our hope of resurrection (see 1 Pet. 3:15). We will be able to share with people out of our entire lives what God has done. The Lord will bless that witness in such a way that people will daily be running to meet the Lord.

As the church in the book of Acts grew, so we will start to see churches grow in our local neighborhoods if we follow the principles laid out earlier in this chapter: gathering together, sharing what we have (both physical and spiritual, including the gifts of the Spirit), spending time with one another besides just on a Sunday morning. Truly living life together will begin to grow the church and bring new people into encounters with the gospel.

The most effective way to introduce people to the saving gospel of Christ is through relationships. Many people can and have attracted others to their churches with a certain type of music, physical setting, the language a pastor uses, or the overall style of a gathering. But as missiologist Eddie Gibbs once said in a meeting with us in Philadelphia, "The unbeliever doesn't care a whole lot about those things; it is the Christian who is looking for a certain type of music or sermon style." Real church growth, based on reaching the unreached, will take place in the church when we simply live the gospel in joyful relationship with one another. That will draw people powerfully.

Do we come to church on Sundays expecting to see new believers changed? We should. That is what the Lord is up to. That is how the Lord met us. We should regularly bring with us to church those who are newborn babes in Christ, introducing them to the body so that we on earth can join with the choir of angels in heaven in rejoicing over this new believer. That is the beginning of a jubilee community. Jesus brought it; and everywhere He went, the jubilee community came behind Him. We carry on His ministry; and everywhere we go, His jubilee community should be coming with us as we introduce the world in which we live to Him.

15

WE CAN DO MORE TOGETHER THAN ALONE

"Evangelicalism" is a confusing contemporary term. Some consider it to be more of a political position than a theological statement of beliefs. The evangelical movement has done some wonderful things, helping individuals understand that they can have a personal relationship with Christ; but it has also had the unintended consequence of causing people to think that this relationship can be maintained independently, apart from the rest of the body of believers. This is the result of the attractional church model in which many, if not most, attendees see fellow believers only on Sunday mornings and rarely during the week—not to mention that it is often possible to attend the Sunday worship service without relating to a single person.

In chapter 10, we focused largely on how believers need each other in the individual church. Now we will examine more fully how that looks in our neighborhoods, inside a network of churches. When Paul wrote his letters to the church in Corinth, he wrote them to a group of believers across that city. It is important to understand that when Paul talked about one body with many parts (see 1 Cor. 12), he was not referring to a single gathering but to a network of believers across the city having all those parts. That information drastically changes the reading of the letter.

At Common Grace, we sometimes find it amusing when we read church mission statements that say something like "our mission is to evangelize, disciple, and train every person in Dallas" or "our vision is to see our church reach its entire community with the gospel of Jesus Christ." While their intention may be good, they are not really possible in isolation. Even the largest churches in the country don't have the capacity to reach more than a small percentage of their communities. And if they did reach more people, where would they put them?

On a trip to Johannesburg, South Africa, I (Coz) drove with my host, Nigel, through the city on a Sunday morning and observed large gatherings of people on the street, many dressed in their church clothes (a type of uniform often identifying which church a person attends). I asked Nigel if the people were waiting to enter a church building. "No," he said. "They can't fit into the building. They have church outside." Sure enough, a few minutes later, we were still driving through this outdoor church when worship began. Despite the large numbers, the group represented but a small fraction of that city's population.

The most troubling aspect of independent mission statements, though, has to do with how churches approach missions in their communities. Churches see reaching their cities as *their* mission rather than the mission of the whole body of Christ and the network of churches in their communities. In such an isolated model, a church has little chance of making progress.

As we saw earlier, isolation produces competition; and competition targets believers in other churches, not the unsaved.

CULTIVATING INTERDEPENDENCE IN THE CHURCH AT LARGE

Recently I (Coz) read a doctoral paper on church succession planning and, although it was excellent overall, one portion of it caught my attention—an argument that the United States' church model of "healthy competition" was a good one. The argument referenced how competition in the capitalistic marketplace keeps businesses focused and accountable. If a business isn't achieving its goals, it will suffer financially and customers will choose a better option. This is true in the church as well, and it wouldn't be a problem if the church viewed the unbeliever as the customer. But the church today often sees the believer as the customer, so we have a consumerist culture fed by Christians looking for a church that satisfies their wish lists. Watching new church plants rapidly grow based on transfers, not new disciples, is a sad thing in communities that are already disjointed.

In this culture and context, we must remember Paul's command to the network of churches in Corinth that we must never say, "I don't need you and you don't need me" (see 1 Cor. 12:21). We need a mutual dependence on one another, not just within our individual churches but across the network of churches in a community and across a city. If we believe that what Paul wrote was a command from God, then we must treat his words that way. A great way to begin applying them is in our church's mission and vision statements: "The mission of our church is to work in conjunction with the other churches in our community to make disciples of every person in our neighborhood." This will move us away from the individualized nature of most churches.

To achieve this goal, we must instill this understanding into the members of our church. Each believer must see themselves as part of the larger body of Christ and part of the church universal. In the Apostles' Creed, which many orthodox churches hold to, the line "We believe in the communion of the saints" is a reference to the idea that we are all part of one body though we bring diversity to the parts of that body.

Many churches invite new believers to become members, asking them to be accountable to the leadership of the church and to make commitments to the church. Other churches don't have membership, since they don't see that in the New Testament. In either case, how much does a local church communicate to its attendees that they are part of a larger body of believers? Not just the local church they attend, not just that denomination or its affiliates, but the entire body of believers around the world? If we can help our congregations see that they are part of the Kingdom, not just a local tribe, then we have the opportunity to fulfill the command in First Corinthians 12. We cannot say we don't need each other. In so doing, we can then work to fulfill the mission of making disciples of all people.

Bishop Eric Lambert of Bethel Deliverance Church in Cheltenham Township, on the outskirts of Philadelphia, understands this idea. When asked about his members, he often responds, "They are not mine; they are God's." He doesn't just speak these words; his strategy plays them out. Bishop Lambert saw early on in his ministry that trying to gather all the people together in one location was inefficient and that the cost needed for buildings to do that could be wasteful. To have a massive sanctuary that sat idle most of the week made no sense to him, so he encouraged his leadership to plant other churches.

In sending out these plants, the mother congregation bears the costs until the daughter congregation is self-sustaining, which is typical of church planters. Bishop Lambert also encourages members of the church to attend the church closest to them; and he especially encourages strong leaders from his church to "leave" the planting church to help build new fellowships, ensuring they have the necessary people to make the new churches effective. This too is common in a healthy church-planting model.

What is unusual, however, is that Bishop Lambert does not restrict his leadership to church plants originating from their own congregation. He also encourages his members to join other churches' plants. Common Grace has sat in meetings in which Bishop Lambert has said to another church planter coming in, "Tell me what you need from us. If it is people, I will be happy to encourage people to join your church."

When asked why he does this, his response captures the idea of a kingdom thinker: "First off, they are God's people, not mine. Who am I to try and hang onto them? Second, I have no doubt that more people will come to our church to fill the spots they leave. We don't have any trouble finding people who don't know Jesus out there. There is no shortage of people for us to reach." Bishop Lambert gets the idea that we are making disciples for the Kingdom, not for our tribes. He ministers without fear that those under his care will leave. If they go on to help the Kingdom grow, praise God!

A similar dynamic takes place at Esperanza Health Center, a medical facility in north Philadelphia that offers affordable, holistic care in Jesus' name. With more than two hundred employees representing more than fifty churches around the region, they find a way to worship God together. Their staff retreats, which take place each quarter, provide a beautiful picture of the Kingdom. The health clinic closes for the day—at a substantial cost to its bottom line—so that the entire staff can be led in the Word of God and pray and praise together. In the room are Presbyterians, Pentecostals, Baptists, Mennonites, and Christian Reformed believers, among others. Worship traditions range from quiet hymns to loud charismatic celebrations, from silent prayer to corporate sharing. Many may be out of their comfort zones, yet in their midst is a sense of being in the house of God. People set aside their own preferences for the opportunity to show unity in mission.

Much of this is because of Esperanza's leadership team: Susan Post, Juan Perez, Brian Hollinger, and Andres Fajardo. They remind the staff of what they all share—the Holy Spirit—and focus on how each person is called to love one another, carry each other's burdens, and be united.

This is particularly evident in Pastor Andres Fajardo, the lead chaplain for Esperanza. He has a congregation outside of Esperanza, the Hunting Park House Church. Pastor Andres is ordained in the Christian Reformed Church and holds to that denomination's doctrinal traditions. At the same time, he is able to pastor the diverse staff at the clinic: affirming the local church that each staff member attends, usually knowing their pastors and having at least a modest understanding of their churches. He doesn't see himself replacing the local pastors but instead enhancing their work. He sees himself as an ally, not a competitor. For this reason, he can celebrate what each church is accomplishing in the kingdom work.

Is it any coincidence that since joining the staff at Esperanza, Pastor Andres now has about thirty volunteer chaplains on board from an array of churches? Once these chaplains meet Pastor Andres, hear his heart, and understand the vision, they too realize that the harvest is plentiful but the workers are few and that together they can accomplish this mission of making disciples in a far more effective way than they ever could alone. Esperanza has more than fifty thousand patient encounters each year. What a field ripe for harvest! But fruit would not be possible without leadership that seeks kingdom gain rather than tribal growth.

The individual local church must see itself as part of the body of Christ in all its diversity. It must recognize that it is not isolated and cannot be effective in isolation. The congregation must also see and celebrate this. It needs to be interwoven into the DNA of a church. This forms the building blocks for community, a sense that we are part of something much bigger than ourselves. When this begins to happen, our local neighborhoods can also be engaged.

How many times do people say, "Why are they planting a new church? We have so many churches as it is" or "There seems to be a church on every corner of our neighborhood." But as we saw earlier, when we break down the number of people in our neighborhoods, the number of churches, and the capacity of each church building, we quickly see that in fact there are not enough churches in our neighborhoods and cities. Usually not even close. What we have is multiple churches competing for the same small group of current churchgoers, and this creates great confusion among unbelievers. Our neighborhoods need to see a unified action on the part of the churches. We already share a unified mission; but if a neighborhood sees churches working strategically together, they will see a kingdom growing and moving forward rather than warring tribes.

WORKING TOGETHER TO REACH EVERY CULTURE

One reason churches need to work together is to help each other relate to the many cultures around them. Many strategies exist to develop community within local churches—small groups, cell groups, men's groups, women's groups, youth groups, midweek services, special events. We can find new and developing terminology around these groups, although in essence they all work to achieve the same thing: intimate fellowship within the gathering of believers. But we should always have a contextual nature to these strategies because different cultures gather in different ways. At times, we must admit that we are not equipped to effectively reach a certain culture; and in those times, we can celebrate the relationships we have with other churches and ministries in our neighborhoods who are equipped to reach them.

Different cultures are not just different ethnic or language groups, but the subcultures within each of those groups. Teenagers gather in a different way than single mothers or young children do. We may be able to intermingle some groups but others will be difficult to blend. In either case, to build community we must be contextual, understanding the culture and how people relate within that culture.

As we begin to understand the culture of the people in our neighborhoods, we should be struck by just how diverse they really are. Unless someone is working in a truly isolated people group (such as a segregated gang population in a prison), most neighborhoods will have a multitude of people groups. As we enter into their worlds and lead our congregations to understand these contexts, new doors will open with the opportunity to make disciples. We may even be surprised at how excited our congregations will become as we engage our neighborhoods.

Churches are not meant to be exclusive clubs for one small part of the population. They should be ever-growing, open to anyone who meets the most basic requirement: faith in Christ. Local churches should not be placed in a location to make it easy for existing members to find parking space; they should be strategically located in neighborhoods where the church can engage its neighbors. To do this, the congregation needs to be taught how to build relationships with the people around them in their everyday interactions and then follow the ripples in the pond.

ONE BODY, MANY PARTS WORKING TOGETHER

Our efforts to reach every culture with the gospel, however, come back to our need to work together as the whole body of Christ. God calls us to work as a unified body.

As I (Coz) walked through Frankford one day with Gabe Wang-Herrera, pastor of a local church called By Grace Alone, he and I discussed what it meant to have a true parish. Pastor Gabe had chosen one of Philadelphia's toughest communities in which to plant a church, an area I mentioned in chapter 4 that I call the "Twilight Zone," jammed full of illegally run boardinghouses as a dumping ground for the prison system.

It was in this community that Pastor Gabe began his church. When the Wang-Herrera family first moved into Northwood, half a dozen blocks from their church in the Twilight Zone, they might as well have been a dozen miles away. People from North-wood "just wouldn't go there." Pastor Gabe had come up with community boundaries; but as we walked around, he realized that they didn't encompass the local high school. "I need to find a way into that place," he commented.

Enter Timoteo Football, which began out of a small church in West Kensington almost a decade ago. With a passion for football, a realization that the needs of the community could not be met by any single church, the understanding that organized sports were limited in the area, and a belief that great things could happen, a small group of churches began developing a flag football competition. Eventually Timoteo grew into a significant network of churches working together to disciple teenagers and young adults in the community. Now with more than two hundred youth, forty coaches and mentors, an "old heads league," camps, websites, all-star games, and awards banquets, Timoteo has become a tool local pastors can use to legitimately make inroads into communities like Frankford and reach unchurched street youth. Gabe became involved with Timoteo and began to connect with his local high school.

The Steelers, the team from By Grace Alone, isn't that good despite the draft and combine that ensures youth from different churches end up playing together. But the lack of ability doesn't stop their dedication, which is evident as you walk by the local park when Ben Soto is running team drills. A few blocks away, the Packers' coaches are working on a playbook. The dominant Eagles are up at six in the morning before school, practicing passing plays. On game day, the crowds build, team jerseys are pulled on, the referees arrive, and the players huddle for prayer. When the game is over, win or lose, everyone gathers in a circle; the coaches remind the players that there is a bigger picture than just this game, that God has a bigger plan, that we are never alone.

"There is one body and one Spirit; . . . one Lord, one faith, one baptism; one God and Father of all, who is over all and through all and in all" (Eph. 4:4–6). Christ has invited us into the unity (see John 17:11) that exists between the Father, the Son, and the Holy Spirit. We have been commanded to "make every effort to keep the unity of the Spirit" (Eph. 4:3). We do not create the unity of the Spirit; our objective is to participate in it—to have fellowship with Christ, even as He has fellowship with the Father, who is in fellowship with the Holy Spirit (see 1 John 1:1–3). We do not invite God into our fellowship—He invites us into His.

Christ is the head of the body, actively administering the affairs of His church (see Eph. 4:11–15) and giving the gift of grace to its members so they will do His work. He does this without discrimination or regard about a person's earthly stature or ability, knowing that no one is deserving of these gifts in his or her own right. Each individual and each church is to use its gifts for the work of the Lord to equip God's people and build up the whole body of Christ (see 1 Cor. 12:7, 11; Eph. 4:11–12; 1 Pet. 4:10) until we obtain the unity of the faith. It is only in working together as one body, with Christ as the head, that we can achieve this purpose of God.

When Paul wrote his first letter to the believers in Corinth, it was not to a single church as we know it but a group of small churches throughout the city. When he spoke to them about unity and body, he was not saying that any one gathering must function as a complete body but rather that all believers and all gatherings must function together without prejudice.

Remember, unity in the body requires us to acknowledge that God is working through unlikely people in unlikely places. In Corinth, Gentiles who had been previously considered "untouchables" were coming into the faith, and Paul enjoined the church not only to accept them but to honor them as they were being honored by God. In John's accounting of Jesus' life, we see Christ speaking with a Samaritan woman, offering her water that would quench her spiritual thirst. Later we see Jesus being anointed by Mary Magdalene, a known prostitute, whom He allowed to touch Him. In the book of Acts, we see Paul, a former persecutor of Christians, commissioned to go to the Gentiles with the good news. In Judges we read of God choosing the weakest family in the weakest tribe to gain the honor of victory in battle through Gideon. God consistently calls us into a unity with other believers that shows no distinction as to worldly status.

RESULTS OF DISUNITY

As we have noted throughout this book, relationships are vital to making disciples in our communities. When we fail to have a humble sense of need for others in the body of Christ, it results in a diminished ability to live incarnational lives in the places where God has called us. When the church fails to function in unity, it becomes impotent, unable to achieve the work of the Lord.

Many churches have taken on a tribal nature. A tribe often sets up walls of protection, expending great energy to shield its small group of people from others. But when churches unite with each other rather than defend their territories, they act as part of God's kingdom with one purpose, unified under one leader.

The failure to unify leads to a poor allocation of resources. Often a number of small churches in one community are all trying to do the same thing, each one working alone. The churches do not affirm one another but rather compete against each other for the handful of believers they gather. While a small percentage of the population is in church each Sunday, most churches spend the majority of their budgets on those who already come to church.

Worship and preaching styles tend to draw believers much more than unbelievers, yet churches use them both to attract attendees, often leading to transfers from other churches rather than unbelievers coming to Christ. When churches discuss joint events, conversation often ends up being about who will get the new people who may begin to attend church as a result of the events.

Large churches tend to give little heed to small churches, rarely inviting them into a true equality of partnership. In doing this, they fail to give honor to the "weaker" parts of the body. Unbelievers and believers are both confused by this sense of competition, in which they seem to be forced to choose sides.

When people travel long distances to a church, usually well outside their communities, they may become disconnected from the work of the Lord going on where they live. Driving somewhere is different from walking there. If we drive, we can speed past the people and problems in a community. If we walk, we must engage our surroundings, no longer in the protective bubble offered by a car.

This disconnection between churches can also lead to a failure to empower local leadership, where often the formally educated become the leaders, overshadowing those from the local communities in a failure to recognize the gifts God has given to the poor.

BETTER TOGETHER

In a recent discussion among a group of pastors in Philadelphia known as Partners in Harvest, one asked, "What could we do together that we cannot do alone?" The twenty or so churches represented in this group ranged in size from a handful of members to more than three thousand gathering on a Sunday, with annual budgets from less than a hundred thousand to multimillions. After some time to consider the matter, the pastor of the largest church spoke about how the churches were not accomplishing all they could alone, that they needed to begin working together, and that they would do great things when they did. He spoke about how many of the churches had day cares operating on shoestring budgets but how together, they could open a Christian school of real size and influence. He spoke about how many of the churches had struggling Bible training programs, but that together they could have a real Bible institute, perhaps a ministry training center. The president of an urban college/ seminary added that perhaps those attending could earn college credit through his institution. Someone else spoke about establishing a home for the elderly, something no one church could accomplish alone.

This conversation didn't develop from a simple question but rather out of years of relationship and building of trust. It didn't come from some magnificent plan laid on the table, a cool PowerPoint presentation, or a crafty speech. It flowed from an understanding of God's call to work together, His command to be unified. It is now being enacted through the humility of pastors who see that the impact that the whole body can have on a city is greater than what their lone tribes can do in a neighborhood.

No part of the human body can survive when it is cut off from the others, and no part of the body of Christ can exist alone. There is only one true church, of which all true believers are a part, and Christ is our head. As Dr. Doug Hall of Emmanuel Gospel Center in Boston writes, "If you want to see change in the system, you first have to be inside the system, living as an integral part of the system in which you are working."[1]

There are no simple formulas for addressing disunity and impotence in the body. It is through relationships—earning the right to speak into the lives of other pastors and their congregants—that fruit is produced. We need to be committed to going into our communities where people live, work, and serve, listening to what God is doing in and through and around them, and encouraging the believers there with stories of others committed to the same things, indwelt with the same Spirit, part of the same body.

Where we live is no accident. God has placed each of us in our communities and called us to live the gospel there—befriending our neighbors, doing life together with members of our local churches, partnering with other bodies of believers in our areas. May we embrace the unity of the Spirit and together bring jubilee to our neighborhoods just as Jesus did, bringing the gospel of hope and deliverance to the poor, the broken, and the lonely in our midst. Place matters.

NOTES

CHAPTER 1: BEING CHURCH IN THE COMMUNITY

1. This idea comes from Dwight Smith of Saturation Church Planting. A number of articles conveying this concept can be found at SCP's website at http://scpglobal.org.

2. "Philadelphia Population 2017," World Population Review, accessed April 19, 2017, http://worldpopulationreview.com/us-cities/philadelphia-population.

3. There has never been an accurate count of church attendance in Philadelphia or even a conclusive count of the number of churches. The estimates Common Grace offers are based on a number of factors and samplings of churches across our city. Studies conducted by the Hartford Seminary Foundation in 2015 and the Duke Divinity School in 1998 and 2006–07 show that 90 percent of churches in the United States with fewer than five hundred attendees account for 50 percent of total church attendance; the remaining 10 percent of churches account for the other half. This and other data lead us to conclude that 178 is the average Sunday morning church attendance in Philadelphia.

4. Our assessment of church decline in the United States comes from our personal observation and Dr. Eddie Gibbs at a consultation of church leaders in Philadelphia in 2004. See also: "7 Startling Facts: An Up Close Look at Church Attendance in America" by Kelly Shattuck published at churchleaders.com in December 2015.

5. Dwight Smith, (Infinity Alliance training seminar, Buffalo, New York, 2005).

CHAPTER 2: CALLED TO DISCIPLE MAKING

1. Dawson Trotman, *Born to Reproduce* (Colorado Springs: NavPress, 1981), 8.

CHAPTER 4: BREAKING DOWN WALLS OF DIVERSITY

1. Steve Daman, "Understanding Boston's Quiet Revival," Emmanuel Gospel Center, October 21, 2016, https://www.egc.org/blog-2/2016/10/13/understanding-bostons-quiet-revival?rq=quiet%20revival.

2. Ram A. Cnaan, *The Other Philadelphia Story: How Local Congregations Support Quality of Life in Urban America* (Philadelphia: University of Pennsylvania Press, 2006); see also Harold Brubaker, "The 'Economic Halo' Effect of Churches," *Philadelphia Inquirer*, December 1, 2016, http://www.philly.com/philly/business/The-economic-heft-of-churches.html.

3. Steven Conn, *Metropolitan Philadelphia: Living with the Presence of the Past* (Philadelphia: University of Pennsylvania Press, 2006), 58.

4. This illustration of Jerusalem's temple is adapted from http://www.biblestudy.org/biblepic/interior-diagram-of-temple-in-jerusalem.html.–Ed.

CHAPTER 6: KNOWING OUR COMMUNITIES' BOUNDARIES

1. Captain Richard H. Pratt, "Kill the Indian, and Save the Man" (1892), History Matters, accessed April 20, 2017, http://history-matters.gmu.edu/d/4929/.

2. Timothy Paul Jones, "The Infamous Evangelical Dropout Statistic: Where It Came from and Why It's a Problem," *Journal of Discipleship and Family Ministry* 3, no. 2 (spring/summer 2013), http://www.sbts.edu/wp-content/uploads/sites/17/2013/10/JD-FM-3.2-Spring-2013-TJones.pdf.

CHAPTER 7: KNOWING OUR COMMUNITIES IN CONTEXT

1. Dr. Eric Mason's Facebook page, accessed April 20, 2017, https://www.facebook.com/Jfthelifechurch.

CHAPTER 9: FROM OUTSIDER TO INSIDER

1. US Census, "Esri Demographics," ArcGIS, accessed April 20, 2017, https://doc.arcgis.com/en/esri-demographics/.

2. Tamar Lewin, "Black Students Face More Discipline, Data Suggests," *New York Times*, March 6, 2012, http://www.nytimes.com/2012/03/06/education/

black-students-face-more-harsh-discipline-data-shows.html; Howard Witt, "School Discipline Tougher on African Americans," *Chicago Tribune*, September 25, 2007, http://www.chicagotribune.com/chi-070924discipline-story.html.

CHAPTER 12: BUILDING RELATIONSHIPS AND TRANSFORMING COMMUNITIES

1. Douglas A. Hall, (lecture, Center for Urban Ministerial Education [Gordon-Conwell Theological Seminary], Boston, 2011); Hall, *The Cat and the Toaster: Living System Ministry in a Technological Age* (Eugene, OR: Wipf & Stock, 2010).

CHAPTER 15: WE CAN DO MORE TOGETHER THAN ALONE

1. Hall, *The Cat and the Toaster*, 71.

PUBLICATIONS

Fort Washington, PA 19034

This book is published by CLC Publications, an outreach of CLC Ministries International. The purpose of CLC is to make evangelical Christian literature available to all nations so that people may come to faith and maturity in the Lord Jesus Christ. We hope this book has been life changing and has enriched your walk with God through the work of the Holy Spirit. If you would like to know more about CLC, we invite you to visit our website:
www.clcusa.org

To know more about the remarkable story of the founding of CLC International we encourage you to read

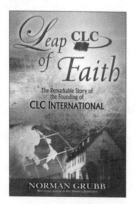

LEAP OF FAITH

Norman Grubb
Paperback
Size 5^1/$_4$ x 8, Pages 248
ISBN: 978-0-87508-650-7
ISBN (*e-book*): 978-1-61958-055-8

NEIGHBOROLOGY

Dr. David S. Apple

Written as a follow-up to *Not Just a Soup Kitchen*, David Apple's *Neighborology* provides a blueprint for how churches and servant leaders of every ministry can be neighborly helpers. Apple provides insight into developing the heart of a servant by modeling the compassion of Jesus Christ and presenting practical instruction and invaluable resources. This book is a must-read for servants of today and tomorrow.

Paperback
Size 5¼ x 8, Pages 193
ISBN: 978-1-61958-239-2
ISBN (*e-book*): 978-1-61958-240-8

NOT JUST A SOUP KITCHEN

Dr. David S. Apple

Not Just a Soup Kitchen is the story of how God transformed the life of the author from near-death skull fracture, childhood sexual abuse, and spiritual bankruptcy to becoming the minister of mercy in the heart of Philadelphia. It is also an instructional guide for those serving in diaconal/mercy ministries.

Paperback
Size 5¹/₄ x 8, Pages 255
ISBN: 978-1-61958-174-6
ISBN (*e-book*): 978-1-61958-175-3